SECRET HORNCHURCH

Carol Cannavan

AMBERLEY

I would like to dedicate this book to my husband, daughter and son, who have been of tremendous support in writing Secret Hornchurch.

First published 2020

Amberley Publishing
The Hill, Stroud
Gloucestershire, GL5 4EP

www.amberley-books.com

Copyright © Carol Cannavan, 2020

The right of Carol Cannavan to be identified as the
Author of this work has been asserted in accordance
with the Copyrights, Designs and Patents Act 1988.

ISBN 978 1 4456 9515 0 (print)
ISBN 978 1 4456 9516 7 (ebook)

British Library Cataloguing in Publication Data.
A catalogue record for this book is available from the
British Library.

Origination by Amberley Publishing.
Printed in Great Britain.

Contents

Introduction

In this book you will discover things about Hornchurch and its people that may surprise you, and will hopefully connect you with its past. Subjects will be covered that you would normally expect to find in a local history book. The difference is, *Secret Hornchurch* aims to dig a little deeper to unearth those little snippets that rarely get mentioned, bringing more depth to our understanding of the past. For instance, the Great Flood of Essex took place in 1888 and covered vast areas of land from Chelmsford and outlying districts all the way to Ilford. Romford was hit particularly hard by the torrential rain; in fact 4.53 inches (115 mm) of rainfall was recorded in just two hours on 1 August 1888. The marketplace and surrounding streets were submerged in 5 feet of water. Romford Brewery suffered a lot of damage. It is estimated that up to 30,000 casks floated away, the majority being empty. Perhaps you knew this, but wonder what that's got to do with Hornchurch? Well, quite a number of those casks were full of beer (newspaper accounts mention 4,000). Many of them were carried for miles by the River Rom. Along the way a large proportion were secured and the contents drank, rendering many completely inebriated. Some ended up in South Hornchurch, where it was reported that, 'free drinking led to very unseemly scenes'. What a hangover that must have been!

You will find that St Andrew's Church is mentioned quite a lot in this book. This is partly due to its age; it is acknowledged to be over 800 years old and is woven into the fabric of Hornchurch. As the parish church, it was central to the community over hundreds of years. If you get the chance, visit the graveyard at the rear. Some of the gravestones are so old you can no longer make out the inscriptions, but many still bear the names of local dignitaries. Two headstones in particular stand out: they are draped with coloured beads and shells, and shared by four men who belonged to the New Zealand Maori Battalion in the First World War.

One of those men, Private Moki, was the son of a ruling chief on the Polynesian island of Niue. He was often referred to as 'Prince Moki'. He died of pneumonia at Grey Towers camp on 30 June 1916, aged twenty-one. Another headstone of interest is partially hidden by shrubs, near to the front of the church. It has a scull and crossbones, and is believed to date back to the sixteenth century. By the way, this doesn't indicate that it is a grave of a pirate; it is a warning to us all that we cannot avoid death and no matter what our status is in life, we are all the same.

Writing this book has been a journey of discovery for me. I hope you feel the same way after you have read it.

Debris from the flood, Romford Brewery. (Havering Libraries – Local Studies)

Above left: The graves of four men from the Maori Battalion.

Above right: Headstone showing scull and crossbones.

1. In the Beginning

Our story begins around 450,000 years ago, when Britain was in the grip of an ice age that almost covered two thirds of its land area. It was known as the Anglian ice sheet and was over a mile thick in places. This powerful force of nature was changing the landscape as it slowly moved from north to south. We know this because the ice sheet transported vast amounts of debris hundreds of miles, ranging from huge boulders (some as large as a bus) to fine rock particles, and deposited them in different geological areas. As the ice melted it left a deposit called 'boulder clay', or 'till', which is a mixture of clay pebbles and boulders.

The Anglian ice sheet had a dramatic effect on the whole of Britain, but most especially it played a crucial role in creating the landscape of London. The evidence lies in a railway cutting adjacent to St Andrew's Park in Hornchurch – it is acknowledged as a Site of Special Scientific Interest (SSSI) and is one of the most important ice age sites in Britain. Back in 1892, the construction of the Romford to Upminster branch line was instrumental in proving that the Thames was diverted to its present course after the arrival of this ice sheet.

At that time T. V. Holmes, a geologist and then vice-president of the Essex Field Club, went to the site and investigated the exposed section, which was around 8 metres deep and 600 metres long. He found around 5 metres thickness of boulder clay occupying a depression in the London Clay, overlain by sand and gravel (known as Orsett Heath Gravel). It is the only place where gravel of the modern Thames comes into contact with glacial deposits.

It is believed that the original course of the Thames was much further north and flowed through central Essex, passing Harlow, Chelmsford, Colchester and Clacton; the coast was not there at the time, but some way out in the North Sea. The Wey and Medway, which flowed through Essex, joined this river. There is some evidence that the Roding and the Ingrebourne would have flowed northwards at the time.

The ice sheet blocked the early Thames and also the tributaries coming from the south. Lakes built up in the tributary valleys, including a small one in the Hornchurch area, fed by water from the rivers and by meltwater from the ice. Eventually, the lakes overflowed, causing the Thames to take a more southerly course. We do not know how long it took for all this to happen, but it was less than 50,000 years.

In 1983, re-excavation of part of a section in the cutting confirmed the site's significance. Geologists now believe that the most southern point of the ice sheet in mainland Britain ended in Hornchurch – at the site where St Andrew's Church stands today.

Many Jurassic fossils were found in the boulder clay, such as ammonites and belemnites, brought here from the Midlands. A vertebra of a plesiosaur, which was a marine reptile, was also uncovered. Plesiosaurs, like dinosaurs lived in the Mesozoic era, which spans from around 252 million years ago to around 66 million years ago.

Hornchurch cutting, a Site of
Special Scientific Interest.

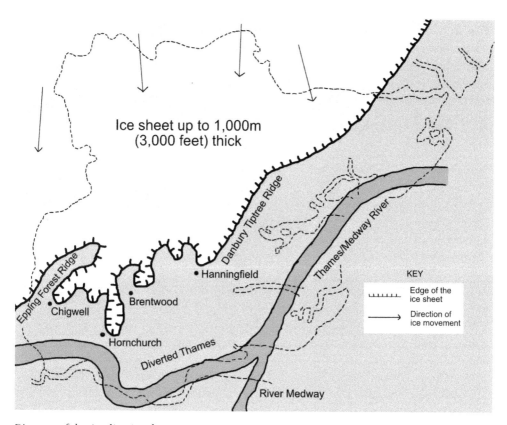

Ice sheet up to 1,000m
(3,000 feet) thick

Danbury Tiptree Ridge

Thames/Medway River

Epping Forest Ridge

Hanningfield

Brentwood

Chigwell

Hornchurch

Diverted Thames

River Medway

KEY

Edge of the
ice sheet

Direction of
ice movement

Diagram of the Anglian ice sheet.

Some time after the ice age, as the climate warmed up, pre-modern humans (Neanderthals and their ancestors) migrated into southern England. These hunter-gathers were unlikely to form settlements as they moved from place to place in search of food. Using wooden spears and stone tools they would have hunted and butchered animals such as antelope, bison, deer and even mammoths. In 1964, remains of a woolly mammoth were found in Sandy Lane Quarry, Aveley, just over 5 miles from Hornchurch. Interestingly, during excavation for the A13 trunk road to the south of Aveley, bones of a range of mammals were found such as brown bear, wolf, giant deer, mammoth, straight-tusked elephant, rhinoceros, horse, bison and a very large lion. It's a fair assumption that these animals would have also roamed the Hornchurch area.

The discovery of Stone Age, Bronze Age and Iron Age tools suggest the area was populated and active thousands of years ago. Many flint objects were recovered during dredging downstream of the Hornchurch Marshes at Long Reach. In South Hornchurch an extensive late Bronze Age settlement was discovered on the Thames terrace gravels. There was evidence of several circular structures, which would have been dwellings, and many items were discovered such as burnt flint, spindle whorls, possible loom weights, a clay sword mould, and plain and decorated pottery. Cremated remains were also found. According to the British Museum, this is the time when sedentary occupation farming first developed.

Roman remains have been found on Mardyke Farm, South Hornchurch, suggesting a settlement once existed there. The Roman road from London to Colchester would have passed through nearby Romford (now the A12).

Modern settlements grew in Anglo-Saxon times from the fifth century. This early medieval period, or Dark Ages, would have been dominated by the nobility and the clergy. It is believed that there was a Saxon church on the site of the present St Andrew's Church (around the year 900).

Flint hand-axe collected by Mr G. R. Ward. (Essex Field Club)

When William the Conqueror was king, he ordered a survey to assess the extent of the land and resources being owned in England at that time. The year was 1086, and Havering is recorded in the Domesday Book as 'Haueringas' and means 'the settlement of the family or followers of a man called Hæfer'. Hornchurch wasn't mentioned. There are records that show that at that time Hornchurch would have been within Becontree Hundred, which was a unit of English local government and taxation. Originally, the term probably referred to a group of 100 hides (units of land required to support one peasant family).

In 1158 Henry II granted the church and land to the monks of St Bernard in Montjoux, reputedly in recognition of the assistance that the Mother Priory of St Bernard in Savoy, Switzerland, gave to royal parties travelling through the Alps. The land stretched from what is now Hornchurch High Street down to Dovers Corner in Rainham, bordered by Abbs Cross Lane in the west and the River Ingrebourne in the east. It is believed that the Hornchurch Priory was built on the north side of the church by the French monks, and was dedicated to St Nicholas and St Bernard. Hornchurch village was probably a small settlement by then. In the bell-ringers' chamber the central light shows Henry II presenting a charter granting land in Havering to a monk from the Abbey of Montjoux.

In 1222, the first written reference to Hornchurch mentions the Monasterium Cornutum, which was known as the horned church at Havering. It's unclear whether the church got its name from its architecture that has been described as having 'horn-like gables', or because of the local leather currying industry, which had either a bull's or a stag's head with horns as its guild sign. On the eastern gable of the chancel is the carved stone head of a Highland bull with hollow copper horns; in the thirteenth century they would have been made from lead. The abbot of the priory used a seal depicting a bull's head, which may be the reason why a horned bull's head was used rather than a cross. There are other stories offering explanations as to how the village got its name, but there is no definitive evidence.

From the thirteenth century onwards Hornchurch was a flourishing community, with at least ten subordinate manors and several farms. In 1465, a charter was granted by Edward IV, exactly 500 years before the London Borough of Havering was formed. The charter gave residents more freedom, such as exemption from paying tolls at markets and bridges, hence the use of the word Liberty. The Liberty of Havering was 9 miles long from north to south and 4.5 miles broad. It consisted of Havering-atte-bower, Romford and Hornchurch. Bordering the Liberty to the west was Becontree Hundred, north was Ongar Hundred and to the east Chafford Hundred, with the Thames in the south at its narrowest point.

After the final years of the medieval kings, the establishment of the new Tudor dynasty heralded a strong economic period locally. The Liberty went on to become a wealthy place of trade and employment encouraging a huge migration of young workers into the area.

The end of the Liberty came in around 1892. In June that year, the final Quarter Session took place in Romford, chaired by Joseph Fry, magistrate, who lived at Fairkytes in Hornchurch. His mother was the famous prison reformer Elizabeth Fry. Two cases were presented. The first involved two tame rabbits being stolen from a Mr Bryant. The defendant, Mr Everitt, was found guilty and sentenced to ten months hard labour. The second case was against Mr Smee, who was accused of stealing two bullocks from

Henry II presenting the charter granting land in Havering.

Bull's head on St Andrew's Church. (© Doug Flack, 2019)

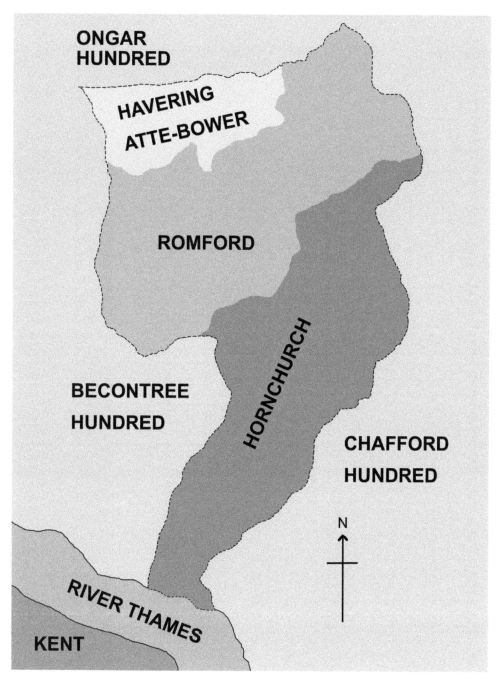

The Liberty of Havering, *c.* 1845.

Mr Rich, a Romford cattle dealer. The accused, a well-know felon, received a sentence of ten years. Joseph Fry was also a founding member of the Metropolitan Drinking Fountains Association.

The grave of Joseph Fry
in St Andrew's churchyard.

Joseph Fry lived at Fairkytes in the late 1800s.

Hornchurch became part of Romford Rural District until 1926, when it became Hornchurch Urban District – this was when the village was recognised as a town. The first meeting took place in April of that year. When the topic of the design of the common seal came up, it was decided to ask Mr Charles Thomas Perfect, 'the historian of Hornchurch', if he would assist in deciding on a suitable design. In 1965 it became part of the London Borough of Havering. Today Hornchurch is a vibrant town and in the 2011 census Hornchurch's population reached 63,583.

DID YOU KNOW?
Tony Robinson narrated a documentary series for Channel 4/National Geographic International called *Birth of Britain*. In the second episode, covering the ice age, Tony visited the railway cutting in Hornchurch. It was broadcast on Channel 4 on 24 January 2011.

2. The Parish of Hornchurch St Andrew

St Andrew's is the parish church of Hornchurch. Its history spans over 800 years. The present building originated in the thirteenth century, although during the fifteenth century the aisles and chancel were rebuilt. The north and south chapels, clerestory, porch and tower were also added around this time. The south aisle and chapel were rebuilt in 1802. Vestry minutes from Romford parish, taken in 1803, describe St Andrew's as the 'church of horn'. A request was made for a contribution from the parishes of Romford and Havering, for the works carried out; at one time they were all part of the parish of Hornchurch. There seems to have been much discussion about this request. Many were of the opinion that although they hadn't received a request for contributions in the past (393 years to be exact), the rate of the contribution was set rather high. However, after seeking advice, it was decided they had to support the Mother Church.

The church is a Grade I listed building, which is built of septaria and ragstone with some brick, and limestone dressing; there is also a fair amount of flint visible. The bull's head, with copper horns, is mounted on the gable of the chancel. The north wall contains a number of bottles, mainly positioned base outwards. These are an interesting addition to the masonry – it's unknown when they were placed there.

The church was included in land granted by Henry II to the monks from St Bernard in Montjoux in 1158. The land comprised the manors of Hornchurch Hall and Suttons (at that time it was worth £25 yearly). The monks would have collected one tenth of annual produce or earnings (a tithe) from any tenants on their land. In 1222 the church was known as 'the horned church' at Havering.

The monks cared for the sick and injured, along with the needs of travellers passing through. Some of these travellers may have been on pilgrimage or on their way to the crusades. Leprosy was a regular feature of life by 1050, so it's likely the monks would have offered food to these poor souls – albeit at a distance as leprosy was greatly feared. Lepers were cast out by the community and would not have been allowed in the church. However, they could view the service being conducted at the altar through a small window set at an oblique angle in the exterior wall. This was known as the Lepers' Squint, a feature that can be found in many medieval churches.

It is known that by 1315 the brethren were struggling and in great poverty. The reason for this is not known, but it is possible that there was a decline in the fertility in the priory's lands, which would have cut their revenue. The downward spiral continued over a number of years. The bubonic plague pandemic that spread through England in 1348 generally resulted in reduced tithes and rents being paid across the land. It's not known how many people were affected or died from the plague in Hornchurch, but London lost almost half of its population – around 40,000 people.

St Andrew's Church, *c.* 1905.

St Andrew's Church. (© Doug Flack, 2019)

Here you can see the bases of several bottles.

Lepers' Squint, on the far right of the photo.

The cylindrical columns date back to the mid-fourteenth century.

The priory survived until it was dissolved by Richard II in 1390/91 when it was sold to William of Wykeham, Bishop of Winchester, to endow his New College in Oxford. He paid 4,000 gold nobles and 500 French francs. This transfer and the appropriation of the church and chapels to New College were confirmed by a papal letter of Pope Boniface IX in 1392. The tower is thought to have been built by William of Wykeham and the fact that it closely resembles New College, Oxford, supports this theory. At the top of the west face of one of the turrets is a seated figure of a bishop believed to represent the Bishop of Winchester. By 1552 five bells were hung in the tower, which would grow to ten by 2000.

The ancient vicarage, known in its later years as the chaplaincy, stood on the north side of High Street. It was built by New College in the financial year 1399–1400. Above the door was the coat of arms of New College, with its motto immortalised by William of Wykeham: 'Manners Makyth Man'. The rectory is believed to have been adapted from priory buildings. Over the years it underwent changes and became known as Hornchurch Hall.

There are no medieval documents in New College's archive referring to the church of Havering/Hornchurch as being dedicated to St Andrew. However, George Reede was instituted vicar of Hornchurch on the feast of St Andrew in 1494. In his will he requested 'to be buried in the Church of St Andrew, Hornchurch'. It may be significant, or simply a coincidence. At that time, New College simply referred to it as 'Ecclesia de Hornchurch'. It is quite possible that it was known informally as St Andrew's before that date. Before the

Bishop at the top of the tower. (© Doug Flack, 2019)

Reformation, the interior of the church would have been brightly decorated with images, unlike the whitewashed walls we see today.

Trinity House, a charity dedicated to safeguarding shipping and seafarers, paid for a lead spire to be added to the tower in 1605 (replaced with copper in 1802). It also contributed an annual peppercorn rent towards the upkeep. At that time the spire played an important role as a navigational aid, used by shipping on the Thames.

To help keep the church in order, a beadle would have been appointed by the vestry (a committee that carried out parochial business). It was the beadle's job to execute the vestry's orders. He was a subordinate to the churchwardens, overseers and constables, which meant the beadle's job was diverse. The beadle served as town crier delivering news, and often solved squabbles between parishioners. At a vestry meeting held on 7 June 1725, Alder Dixon was selected as beadle. His salary as vestry clerk and beadle was £4 per annum. The Overseers of the Poor agreed to buy him a large coat to cover his clothes and a hat.

The church was lucky to escape major damage during the Second World War, but the east window was destroyed by enemy action and was replaced. The five-light Perpendicular window is dedicated to the memory of Thomas Mashiter (1780–1862), who was High Steward of the Liberty of Havering and a Justice of the Peace. It was designed by Gerald Smith and made by Nicholson Stained Glass Studio in 1954.

The window dedicated to Thomas Mashiter.

The Clergy

When New College, Oxford, was endowed with the church and its lands, it appointed a vicar temporal to be their 'Ordinary', as the Book of Common Prayer would have expressed it. As a result of this, the incumbent of Hornchurch enjoyed freedom from the jurisdiction of the bishop. This was called a 'Peculiar', which ended in 1901. Before 1901 the bishop had to ask permission to enter the church. New College is still involved with the bishop in appointing the incumbent.

In 1531, Revd Thomas Duke was installed as chaplain. A few years later, in 1534, Henry VIII broke away from the Catholic Church and was declared 'Supreme Head on Earth of the Church of England'. Following on from this, monasteries and religious houses were closed and their buildings, land and money taken by the Crown. It is said that the Revd Duke was outraged by this and was accused of sending treasonous letters and organising a plot to kill the king. The outcome of these allegations is not known. However, it's likely that nothing was proved as the next Chaplain to take over in St Andrew's was Richard White, who was installed some years later in 1540, which indicates the Revd Duke was still in office. It is said that Thomas Duke was a wealthy man and had powerful friends – that could have gone in his favour.

An incredible number of chaplains, vicars and curates have served the church over its long history. Revd William Henry Reynell was one of the longest serving chaplains. He became chaplain in 1768 and remained at St Andrew's until he died in 1809, a total of forty-one years. His wife Martha died four years later in 1813. They had two children, but Thomas died in infancy and Walter died in 1824 aged twenty-nine years. There is a memorial plaque for Reynall inside the church.

In February 1776, The *Norfolk Chronicle* reported the following incident:

> Last Sunday week, at night, Rumford church in Essex, was broke into and robbed of thirty shillings and two-pence, sacrament money; the plate was in the church, but the thieves did not find it. Hornchurch church was likewise broke into the same night, and the box broke open where the writings were kept, several of which, and the great bible, were rent, but the thieves found nothing worth taking away.

The ancient bible, dating back to the seventeenth century, is still in the care of St Andrew's Church. It is amazing to think that at one time Revd Reynell would have read from this book as he preached to the congregation.

Revd Herbert Dale, vicar for sixteen years (1902–18), was held in high esteem by his parishioners. His name is carved in the bench in the lychgate. When he resigned in 1918 because of ill health, he was presented with a packet of war bonds to the value of £216 – the equivalent today would be around £11,500 and his wife received a canteen of silver.

His son, Captain Philip Dale, who served with the Essex Regiment, was taken prisoner in the First World War and was imprisoned in Ludwigshafen. On his fifth attempt, he managed to escape to Holland. He reached home on Sunday 12 May 1918 – one week after his escape from the camp. He had the honour of being received by the king at Buckingham Palace, and was later awarded the Military Cross for his hazardous venture.

Revd Charles Steer also had the misfortune to be a prisoner of war. He served as a chaplain in the trenches, and was a former curate at St Edward's Church in Romford.

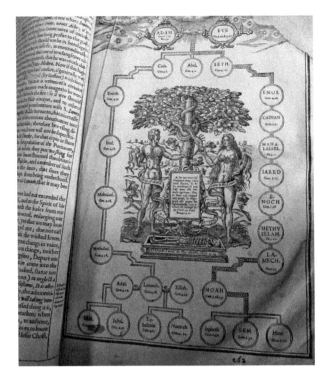

The seventeenth-century bible of St Andrew's Church.

The bench in the lychgate commemorating Revd Herbert Dale.

Because he was a non-combatant, the Germans released him and soon after he was appointed vicar of Hornchurch (1918–25).

In 1969 the chaplaincy (now Chaplaincy Gardens) was sold and demolished in 1970 – three-storey flats now stand on this site. The house at No. 222 High Street, which is adjacent to the church, is now used as the parish office.

Many prominent people who lived and died in Hornchurch have been laid to rest in St Andrew's graveyard. The brethren from the priory would have had wooden crosses, which would have rotted away hundreds of years ago. However, under the fitted carpet in the chancel there is a memorial floor slab for Boniface de Hart, who was prior from 1323 to 1325. The ravages of time have made it impossible to read the inscriptions on many of the headstones in the graveyard, but there are many from the nineteenth century whose names are linked to people who helped to shape Hornchurch. There are a number of memorials inside St Andrew's dedicated to members of the church, prominent members of the community, and those who lost their lives in wartime. In the sanctuary is the Ayloffe table tomb, which dates from the sixteenth century.

Other churches in the parish of Hornchurch St Andrew include St George's Church, Kenilworth Gardens (built 1930) and St Matthew's Church, Chelmsford Drive (built 1956). In 1928 St Andrew's bought the redundant village school in North Street as a place of service to the community. Today, various groups meet in the North Street Halls, and in 2011 it became home to the Messy Church. Hornchurch itself is home to around twenty places of worship of various denominations.

The Chaplaincy, *c.* 1960s. (Havering Libraries – Local Studies)

William Ayloffe lived at Bretons. He died in 1517.

DID YOU KNOW?

In 1999 the copper horns were stolen from the bull's head on the eastern gable of the chancel. They were never recovered and new horns replaced them in 2001. In 2011, St Andrew's Church had copper stolen from the roof ten times in five months. An alarm was fitted to the roof, but thieves managed to get around it, so the vicar, organist and eight parishioners took it in turns to sleep in the church until the alarm system could be extended.

3. The Workers

Leather was at the heart of Hornchurch's commercial life for hundreds of years. The stone-carved head of a bull on St Andrew's Church may be an indication of how important the leather trade was to the community. Another indicator was the name of the road running through the centre of the village in the thirteenth century, which was known as Pell (or Pelt) Street – now High Street. Hornchurch would have had fellmongers, tanners and curriers. Fellmongers usually worked with smaller skins, particularly sheep. It was their job to separate the wool from the pelts. Tanners used a process that permanently altered the protein structure of skin, making it less likely to decompose. Curriers were involved in the process of stretching and finishing tanned leather, rendering it supple and strong for the use of a saddler or shoemaker.

A reminder of the ancient leather industry in Hornchurch.

Working in a tannery wasn't a pleasant occupation. It was backbreaking work and the smell would have been overpowering as in the early days pigeon and dog faeces would have been used along with urine. The last tannery, that of Bright & Beardwell in High Street, closed around 1846. James Fry of North Street worked in Hornchurch as a fellmonger – his business closed around 1870.

Romford had a market by 1247. Initially it sold livestock and opened one day a week – Wednesdays. Over the years market days increased, and so did the variety of goods on sale. By the fifteenth century the market was widely known for the sale of leather goods made in Hornchurch. These would have included harnesses, saddles, shoes, boots, gloves, breeches, jackets and jerkins. Romford was particularly well known for producing leather breeches, so there would have been a high demand for skins to be supplied from Hornchurch.

Each year the court leet – a court for non-criminal offences and appointment of officers – would appoint Searchers and Sealers for Leather. This is a role that went back to Tudor times. It was their job to make sure that the leather was being sold at an appropriate price, was cured properly and was of good quality. They would select a number of skins/hides and feel the quality and thickness, and then smell the leather to check its tanning. If they were satisfied, they would give the seller a sprig of evergreen to hang over their portal and would issue a certificate. If their leather didn't make the grade they were fined. William Young and William Webber were appointed Searchers and Sealers for Leather for Hornchurch by Romford magistrates at the Whitsun Court Leet in May 1733.

Romford Market, *c.* 1905.

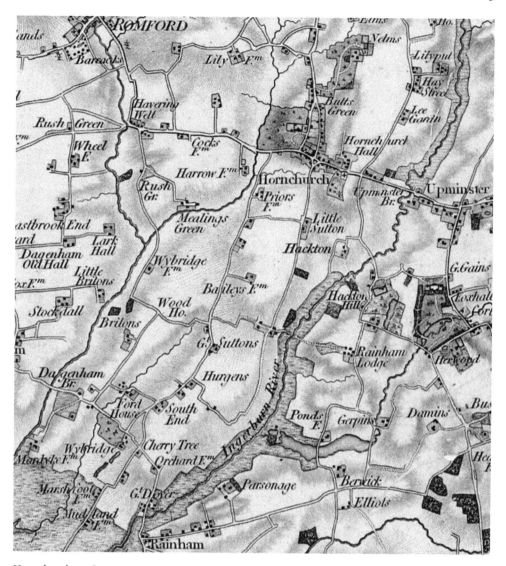

Hornchurch, c. 1805.

Farming would have been the main occupation in Hornchurch from medieval times up until the twentieth century. Common crops produced in the Middle Ages included wheat, beans, barley, peas and oats. Charles Perfect, the local historian, wrote the following in his book *Ye Olde Village of Hornchurch*:

In July 1812, a return was made to Parliament, which gave the following particulars: Inhabited houses – 286, uninhabited – 8, families chiefly employed in agriculture – 197, families employed in trade and manufacture – 80.

At that time there were 1,567 people living in the area. By 1848 there were over twenty farms in Hornchurch. Farming remained the main profession in Havering until after the First World War.

Before the days when milk was delivered to the door, customers would collect it in jugs or cans from local farms or dairies and use it that day. It wasn't until mid-Victorian times that milk was delivered direct to the customer. In some areas it would have been delivered twice a day, especially in the summer months, because there was no refrigeration. The milk seller carried the milk in large urns in a horse-drawn, two-wheeled cart, and would ladle the milk into jugs. The cart became know as a float as it carried milk. When the old float carts were replaced with the electric vehicles, the name 'milk float' remained. The first glass milk bottles started appearing in the 1880s in the UK. By the end of the nineteenth century milk had emerged as the most important single item sold off English farms.

Richard Banyard ran his dairy farm on the land of Little Nelmes in the late 1800s. It is said that in the early days of Emerson Park it wasn't unusual to see two or three of Banyard's cows happily munching on garden shrubs. In 1903 he paid £220 rent for the farm per annum and an additional £54 rent for pastureland. He had depots at No.19 North Street, Hornchurch, and No. 64 Victoria Road, Romford. Although of good character, he was summoned before magistrates in October 1905 for selling milk that was 23 per cent deficient in milk fat. Mr Banyard said he could only account for the deficiency by the fact that September was a poor month – he did all he could to produce the best milk. Although the magistrate had sympathy for Mr Banyard, he was fined 20s with costs of 4s.

Milkman (unknown) delivering in Emerson Park, *c.* 1920. (Upminster Tithe Barn)

Milkman posing with bottles of milk,
c. 1920. (Upminster Tithe Barn)

Banyard lived on the farm with his wife, three sons and three daughters. In *The Story of Ardleigh Green* by J. B. Warren, it mentioned a letter sent to a Mr Peter Radling in January 1923 from Banyard, offering him work. The hours were 5.15 a.m. to 5.50 p.m. with one hour for breakfast and one and a half hours for lunch, seven days a week. Banyard offered 8*d* an hour wages for weekdays and 10*d* per hour for Sundays. 5*s* per week would be deducted for a pint of milk and rent of a house.

There were three corn mills in Hornchurch in the thirteenth century: a watermill on the manor of Dovers, which existed until 1614; a windmill on the manor of Mardyke; and a windmill in Mill Field, near to St Andrew's Church. The Mardyke windmill was replaced in the sixteenth century with a post mill – there was no mention of it by 1777. The windmill in Mill Field was rebuilt twice; once in 1564, but there was no sign of it by 1618, then it was rebuilt as a post mill around 1666. It was still in use by 1912. On a particularly hot day in June 1921 it burnt down.

Hornchurch became a centre of excellence in the form of agricultural equipment in the early nineteenth century. Two brothers, Thomas and Robert Wedlake, opened the Fairkytes Iron Works in Billet Lane around 1809. At first they traded as millwrights – today they would have been called engineers. Their inventions, which were mainly improvements on agricultural equipment, made a huge impact on farming, cutting down on manpower and horses. They won various awards, medals and certificates of distinction from the British Society of Agriculture for their ploughs, haymaking

THE MILL. HORNCHURCH

Post mill near to St Andrew's Church, *c.* 1900.
(Upminster Tithe Barn)

machines, turnip cutters and threshing machines. To show their appreciation, agriculturalists gathered in the White Hart in August 1833 and presented a silver tea urn, weighing 160 ozs, to Thomas Wedlake.

The brothers' name spread as emigrant farmers going to Australia, New Zealand and other British colonies bought equipment to take with them. At their peak of prosperity they employed eighty or ninety people at a dozen forges. The census in 1821 shows an increase in the population in Hornchurch by 373 people (1,938 in total). When comparing with other years, before and after, it's likely that the iron foundry attracted more people into the area at this time when they were building up the business.

When Thomas died in 1843, his widow Mary took over the business with her daughter Eliza and son-in-law Louis Philip De Porquet, trading as Mary Wedlake & Co. His younger brother, Robert, discovered that Thomas had not signed his will, which meant he no longer had any right to share the past profits. It is obvious by the notice he placed in the *Essex Herald* in October 1843 that he was very upset by the situation. In response, he decided to set up the Union Foundry in High Street, next to the Bull Inn, with a new partner, Mr Thompson. Mary Wedlock died in 1846, but the ironworks continued until 1855 when it went out of business. Robert Wedlake died in 1864. His son-in-law Richard Dendy purchased the Union Foundry around 1861, after Robert had retired. Robert's son Thomas W. Wedlake became a partner but by 1894 the partnership ended. Richard

A **GENTLEMEN**

A **FTER** Thirty-five Years Co-operation with my late lamented Brother, Thomas Wedlake, I have received notice from the surviving members of his family, Mrs. Wedlake and Mons. Louis de Porquet, to withdraw from an Establishment which has had the benefit of my Inventions, and to the interest of which my best years, since its foundation, have been devoted.

The suddenness of my brother's death has deprived me of all participation in the profits which the past has realized : his sense of justice and his kindness of heart, had he signed his will, would have given to me a fair share; but now I am unexpectedly thrown upon my generous countrymen and my own resources for the support of myself and family. Therefore, Mr. Thompson, my friend in adversity, and myself, will, as Co-partners, and without loss of time, OPEN A NEW FACTORY, in HORNCHURCH, to be named "THE UNION FOUNDRY."

The death of Thomas Wedlake caused a family dispute.

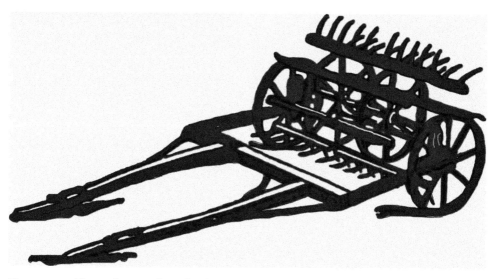

The renowned haymaking machine developed by the Wedlake brothers.

Dendy's son, Walter, took over the business and transferred the Union Foundry to Barking in 1902, renaming it the London Scottish Foundry.

Thomas W. Wedlake lived in the White House on the east side of North Street, formerly known as Grosvenor House. It was built around 1700 and was eventually destroyed by fire and demolished in 1957.

It is believed that there were brewers in Hornchurch in 1583 and 1606, but it wasn't until 1789 that the Hornchurch Brewery was established by John Woodfine. His son Thomas was involved with developing the site, and when he died his son, also Thomas, took over running the business. The brewery was sold to Henry and Benjamin Holmes in 1874. Charles Dagnall was the next buyer. He formed the Old Brewery Company in 1889, but wasn't very successful.

When Philip Conron bought the business in 1892 it had thirty-six licensed inns and beerhouses in the district. Conron was determined to make a success of the business. Part of that would have been keeping his workers happy. A short report was put in the *Dagenham Gazette* in September 1898, describing their autumn 'beanfeast' trip:

> The employees of the Old Hornchurch Brewery travelled from London Bridge to Brighton in a saloon carriage. After visiting the pier, pavilion, aquarium, and other places of interest, a move was made for the Unicorn Hotel, where a substantial repast was provided. In a speech, Mr Conron said that they had had a year of unprecedented prosperity...

The White House after the fire. (Upminster Tithe Barn)

OLD HORNHCURCH BREWERY

Brewers Wine and Spirit Importers

HORNCHURCH

India Pale and Mild Ales, Nourishing Stout
and Porter in Cask and Bottle

**Speciality : Haughs O'Cromdale Pure Malt Scotch
Whisky (8 years old) 3s. 6d. per Bottle**

Agencies: SIR JOHN POWER'S DUBLIN WHISKY (7 years old)
3/- per Bottle, (10 years old) 3/6 per Bottle

**Louis Massenet Reims Champagne (Old Landed)
Excellent Value 3s. 6d. per Bottle.**

Deliveries in Grays, Purfleet, Aveley, and Rainham daily.

The advert that appeared in local newspapers in 1903.

Beanfeast is an informal term for a celebratory meal or party, especially an annual summer dinner given by an employer to their employees – it was later known as 'Beano'. He also used the newspapers to advertise his offerings – such as the one placed in the *Grays & Tilbury Gazette* in July 1903. In 1925, the brewery was taken over by Messrs Mann, Crossman and Paulin but brewing ceased there in 1929.

The Workhouse

In 1598, four cottages that were known as Pennant's Almshouses were bequeathed for the use of the poor in the parish. They were situated on the corner of High Street and Billet Lane – now Sainsbury's. They were used for this charitable purpose until 1721 when they were demolished and the site was used to build the Hornchurch workhouse. Private benefactors built almshouses, whereas workhouses were built by the parish and had strict rules. Inmates could expect to work up to a twelve-hour day and in return would be clothed and fed. If they refused to work or were disruptive, they would go without food. Any profit from the work carried out would be kept by the workhouse master.

By the early 1800s there were forty inmates in the Hornchurch workhouse. One of the back bedrooms was partitioned to accommodate anyone who was deemed insane. This was a temporary measure, as they would be transferred to the Bethnal Green Madhouse. The vestry would be charged for keeping insane residents in the asylum. In October 1826, a Mrs Hampton petitioned the select vestry asking how she was suppose to support her children after her husband was put in the workhouse. She was refused relief on account of spending her earnings on gin.

In the later years, life probably wasn't too bad in the workhouse as in September 1835 it was reported that:

> There are at this time in Hornchurch workhouse, eight men whose united ages amount to 634 years, also five women whose ages amount to 412, the youngest of whom is eighty-one.

The workhouse came to the end of its use in August 1836, when the furniture was sold off, including twenty feather beds. It closed in 1837 and was converted back into almshouses. They were destroyed by fire in the late 1970s.

DID YOU KNOW?
In 1938, workmen widening the road from Hornchurch to Upminster at a section opposite St Andrew's Church found a hoard of coins (now known as the Hornchurch Hoard). It consisted of 448 medieval silver pennies, two short cross pennies, ten Irish pennies, twenty-one Scottish sterlings and four forgeries. Some were struck the same year that Romford Market was founded in 1247, which means it's quite possible that the first market traders handled some of these very coins.

4. Drink Up!

Over the centuries there were plenty of opportunities for the residents of Hornchurch to quench their thirst. The monks at the priory, back in the twelfth century, would have brewed their own ale. It would have been made with grain, water and fermented with yeast – basically a sort of barley soup – nothing like the clear beer that is brewed today. It provided hydration as well as some nutrition and because it could be brewed in a few days it was only mildly alcoholic, so children could drink it. In the medieval period, access to clean water couldn't be guaranteed, so ale was the preferred drink.

By the end of the fifteenth century, hops were being cultivated in Kent. Hops give beer flavour and, most importantly, they keep it from going off. The shelf life for ale brewed without hops can be as short as a fortnight or so before it starts to spoil and sour. Hopped beer can last for years. This was good news for 'Ale Conners'. The ale conner had to test the quality and strength of beer, and ensure it was sold at a fair price. He also had the authority to impose fines. Surprisingly, it wasn't a popular or sought-after position. There are numerous records from early London demonstrating that ale conners were often fined for not performing their duties. The risk was becoming ill, or even dying from what they drank. This may well be the reason that one method they used for testing the quality was to pour a little ale onto a wooden bench and sit in it for half an hour or so. Apparently, they made a judgement on how sticky their leather breeches were to assess the alcoholic strength of the ale, and would then impose the appropriate duty. Ale conners would be appointed at a court leet for a period of one year. Frederick Powling was appointed ale conner for Hornchurch by Romford magistrates at the Whitsun Court Leet in May 1863. Four ale conners are still chosen annually by the Common Hall of the City of London.

In 1762, there were eight inns open in the parish of Hornchurch, including Harold Wood. Four of them were in the village. Many of the inns were also used as venues for inquests. The oldest in the village was the White Hart. The original inn is thought to have dated back to around the fifteenth century, possibly earlier, but that burned down on 7 November 1872. The landlord at the time, Mr Elliott, his wife and ten children were all in bed asleep when the fire broke out. The smell of smoke and the sound of crackling wood woke them up. As they tried to escape they found the stairs were destroyed, so they shouted out of the windows for help. Luckily, aid soon arrived, and a platform was placed beneath the window, which allowed a number of men to reach the children and get them to safety. Thankfully, they all got out alive. A mounted messenger was despatched to Romford and the brewery engine arrived relatively quickly, but water could only be obtained from a small tap. At the time, there were wooden-framed cottages that surrounded the inn, so they also had to be doused with water; there was only a light breeze though, which helped to limit the damage. Only one cottage that immediately adjoined the rear of the inn premises was burnt, but those on the other side survived, but

The Victorian White Hart building, *c.* 1910. (Havering Libraries – Local Studies)

'the glass cracked, the paint blistered and the tar melted'. Many of the cottagers sustained great loss in trying to remove goods from their houses. 'In a short time the roof of the White Hart fell in with a tremendous crash' – the fire was still smouldering the next day. Nothing remained of the building except half of the clubroom, two chimneys facing the street and the stables, which were in the rear.

The replacement building was a functional Victorian brick-built hotel, supplied by Ind Coope and Co. Ltd of Romford. In 1935 the building was replaced once more when road widening took place at the junction of Station Lane and the High Street. It underwent many name changes over the years: Madison Exchange, Newt and Cucumber, and Lloyds No. 1 (a subsidiary of Wetherspoon's). It eventually closed in 2006. Today, the building has been divided into several restaurants, but locals still refer to it as the White Hart.

The King's Head in High Street dated from 1680 and was originally a coaching inn. It also staged cockfights. A notice went into the *Ipswich Journal* on 26 March 1763, advertising matches between fighting cocks to take place at the King's Head on 28–30 March at eleven o'clock in the morning and four o'clock in the afternoon. The matches had been arranged by the Gentlemen of Essex and the Gentlemen of London and comprised fifty-one cocks for the main bouts (these were based on the weight of the birds) and fifteen 'byes' (lesser battles of different weights). The purse was five guineas a battle, and fifty the odd battle; the odd is the final battle between the largest birds, which determines the overall champion – hence the higher wager. Fifty guineas was a tremendous amount of money in those days – the average annual income for a typical workingman was £20.

The King's Head, *c.* 2000. (Upminster Tithe Barn)

From 1789, the King's Head was owned by the Old Hornchurch Brewery, which was situated opposite the building. The bottling plant was next door. Workers at the brewery had a daily allowance of five pints of beer, which had to be taken at the King's Head.

The building has had many alterations, inside and out, over the years. In 1926 the old oak-beamed ceilings were removed, along with the original fireplace, which was said to be enormous. A fire in 1966 led to further alterations. The King's Head closed in 2007, but the building is still in use. It is now a Prezzo restaurant.

The Bull Inn, situated in High Street (now the Fatlin), was rebuilt in 1953. The original inn is thought to have been built sometime in the sixteenth century and had various building works carried out over the centuries. One of the long-serving landlords, George Heath, also served as a jobmaster, hiring out carriages and carts. He employed a cabman called Harry Wooley, who lived in North Street. In October 1900, Wooley was with his helper, a twelve-year-old boy named John Rolph, when the horse suddenly bolted. Wooley desperately hung on, but he eventually became exhausted and fell. One of the wheels ran over his back and killed him – he left a widow and three children. John Rolph, who was riding on the load, was thrown and his left leg was broken. He was taken to Romford Victoria Cottage Hospital. The inquest actually took place in the Bull Inn and must have been especially difficult for George Heath. Dr Ryan said death resulted from rupture of the liver. The jury returned a verdict of 'accidental death', and expressed the opinion that the deceased met his death in trying to prevent the boy from being injured.

The Good Intent in South Hornchurch was a popular pub with the airmen and ground crew at the Royal Flying Corps Station Suttons Farm during the First World War, and

The Bull Inn, *c.* 1910. (Havering Libraries – Local Studies)

Good Intent pub sign showing Spitfires.

RAF Hornchurch in the Second World War. Operating as a beerhouse in the early 1800s, it became the Good Intent in 1851. It was bought by the Old Hornchurch Brewery in 1910 and sold to Mann and Crossman in 1925. It was rebuilt in 1927.

The Harrow Inn, in Hornchurch Road, is dated from 1894. However, another building of that name stood on the same site, possibly in the seventeenth century. The Beerhouse Act (1 Will. IV, c.64 1830), was introduced by the Duke of Wellington's Tory government. It abolished the beer tax and extended the opening hours of licensed public houses, taverns and alehouses to eighteen hours a day. Previously it was fifteen hours. This suited farmers and hay carters on their way to the London market. Around three o'clock in the morning, they would arrive at the Harrow Inn for refreshments, sometimes in a convoy. Nosebags would be put on the horses and the drivers would congregate inside. Sometimes, they would bring steak and cook it on the tap-room fire.

Although the law may have been lax when it came to opening hours in the 1800s, it could be harsh if you overindulged. In November 1880, Bridgett Ellen Wolfe, who had been repeatedly before the bench for being drunk and disorderly in Hornchurch, was sentenced to twenty-one days hard labour!

Billet Lane takes its name from the Crooked Billet, a public house that opened in 1828 and closed around 1874. The building itself was considerably older, possibly 300 years old. It was demolished in 1917 and in its place a residence was built, which was known as The Billet. Currently, it is used by Fairkytes, Havering's arts centre.

The Harrow, *c.* 1910. (Havering Libraries – Local Studies)

The Billet – now used as an arts centre.

Britannia was opposite the Archway, *c.* 1900. (Upminster Tithe Barn)

The Chequers Inn, *c.* 1905.

Another short-lived establishment was the Britannia, which was located on the corner of North Street, roughly opposite where the sixteenth-century Archway was sited. Again, it was housed in a building that was extremely old. After being used as a beerhouse for around forty-two years its licence was withdrawn in 1907, on the grounds that it was 'dated and inferior, was difficult for supervision, and would not justify any large amount being laid out on it'.

The Cricketers Inn was located on High Street, dating back to the seventeenth century. It had dangerously low ceilings, and was demolished in 1938. The Spencer's Arms, Ardleigh Green, existed for at least 200 years before a couple of name changes and renovations, and is now called The Ardleigh. The Crown in Hornchurch Road, on the border of Romford, was rebuilt in 1923. It is thought that the original building dated back to the fifteenth century. The Chequers Inn on North Street, where Billet Lane leads into Butts Green Road, was rebuilt in 1899. It replaced another inn of the same name previously there.

DID YOU KNOW?
At the beginning of August in 1888, torrential rainfall caused severe flooding in many parts of Essex, including Havering. The main street near the Hornchurch Brewery was covered with several feet of water. Some of the adjacent dwellings had floors below the level of the road, and the occupants were rescued from the bedroom windows by carts. Near the Bridge House (now The Windmill), on the border of Upminster, half the roadway was washed away for a considerable distance. The culvert, which carried the road over the River Ingrebourne was severely damaged.

5. Shadows of the Past

In Hornchurch we are lucky to still have some wonderful buildings that date back hundreds of years. Among them are public houses, residences and, of course, St Andrew's Church. Some notable buildings are still standing, but are used in a different capacity, including Langtons (registry office and wedding venue), Fairkytes (arts centre), Duryfalls (now apartments), Harrow Lodge (mental health centre) and Bretons in South Hornchurch (outdoor recreation centre).

Wykeham Cottage is an example of some of the buildings that once formed the old village of Hornchurch. Dating from the eighteenth century, this timber-built cottage is a Grade II listed property. In the early to mid-nineteenth century, a room was used as a courthouse.

Wykeham Cottage is a Grade II listed building.

Some buildings may have been demolished, but they still have a place in history, brought to life by the stories of the people associated with them. One such building was Hornchurch Hall, which, although altered over the years, had its roots going back to the beginning of the fifteenth century.

After the monks of St Bernard arrived in 1158, they erected priory buildings. Over the centuries these buildings underwent many changes. A chaplaincy was built around 1400, situated quite near to the rectory. New College, Oxford, built a dividing wall between the two buildings in the fifteenth century and leased out the rectory manor, which entitled a lessee to collect tithes. The rectory eventually became known as Hornchurch Hall. The building continued to be updated through the centuries and although the south façade of the hall was Victorian, other parts of the building dated from the sixteenth century. The estate comprised 306 acres, falling to 280 acres by 1849 – 145 acres being arable and 143 acres of pastureland. New College sold all the Hornchurch Hall land for development between 1927 and 1931. Hornchurch Urban District Council bought some of it, and the British Land Company and Mr Robert Beard were among other purchasers. The house was damaged by bombing in 1940 and was demolished in 1941. Today, the site is occupied by the Olive AP Academy Havering, replacing the Robert Beard Centre.

Hornchurch Hall had many prominent people associated with it over the years. However, one man stands out from the rest, for all the wrong reasons. John Ward of Hackney leased Hornchurch Hall in the early part of the eighteenth century. Documents also show that in 1718 he bought four farms and land in Hornchurch for £794. He was a

THE HALL. HORNCHURCH

Hornchurch Hall, *c.* 1910.

very wealthy man, and his main residence in Hackney was substantial. In 1722 he was a Member of Parliament for Weymouth – many say this was achieved by bribery and corruption. In 1725 he became involved in a dispute with the executors of the late Duke of Buckingham, from whom in 1705 he had leased some alum works in Yorkshire. The nineteen-year lease required the duke to buy 740 tons of alum a year, and Ward offered to store it until the price increased. However, Ward sold it on the open market, which resulted in him being paid twice for it, once by the purchaser and once by the duke. He managed to swindle £70,000 from the duke, of which only £10,000 was recovered. When the lease expired the duke's executors acted on behalf of the new duke, a minor. Ward had failed to comply with a covenant requiring him to leave 351 tons of alum at the end of the term, so the executors instituted proceedings in Chancery against him. His defence was that he had been released from this covenant by a note from the duke. However, this was proved to relate to another matter and had been altered by Ward to suit his purpose. He was found guilty of forgery and expelled from the House of Commons. Ward promptly absconded and managed to evade justice for eight months. In February 1727 he was fined £500 and was sentenced to stand in the pillory for an hour.

That wasn't his only brush with the law. Some time later he was imprisoned for concealing his wealth, estimated at £150,000. This came about because of his involvement with Sir John Blunt, who created what has become known as one of history's most extreme cases of stock market speculation and manipulation, involving the South Sea Company. Eventually Ward surrendered himself to the bankruptcy commissioners. It is said that during his confinement in 1732, Ward amused himself by giving poison to dogs and cats, then watching them expire 'by slower or quicker torments'. He was involved in a string of questionable schemes and money lending throughout his life. He died 30 July 1755, predeceased by his only son, Knox Ward.

Among his papers a prayer was found, written by John Ward (date unknown), which went on to be published in many newspapers under the title 'A Miser's Prayer'. Here is a short extract:

o Lord, thou knowest that I have nine houses in the City of London, and likewise that I have lately purchased an estate in simple-fee in the county of Essex. I beseech thee to preserve the two counties Middlesex and Essex from fire and earthquakes; and as I have a mortgage in Hertfordshire, I beg of thee likewise to have an eye of compassion on that county; and for the rest of the counties thou mayest deal with them as thou art pleased ...

Another unique building was Grey Towers. Whereas Hornchurch Hall had a rich history spanning over 540 years, Grey Towers only existed for just over fifty years. However, Henry Holmes, who built it in 1876, became an indispensable member of the community and was held in great esteem.

Previously, he and his wife Emilie and their six children had lived in Harwood Hall in Corbet's Tey, Upminster. Grey Towers shared a lot of similarities with the Upminster property, including its castellated style. Initially, the land was part of the Langtons estate, which was owned by his father-in-law John Wagener. Holmes bought 87 acres from him. Grey Towers must have been an impressive building, with its castellated lodges and

John Wagener was buried in St Andrew's churchyard in 1884.

landscaped gardens leading down to the ornamental lake. In later years it was completely covered by creepers and ivy.

Henry Holmes came from an old and influential Durham Quaker family. Son of a north-country shipbuilder, he had shipyards in Middlesborough and was a director of the London City and Midland Bank. While living at Grey Towers, Holmes ran the Hornchurch Brewery with his brother Benjamin. He soon became immersed in local affairs. There is a long list of his involvement with community matters: he was the first chairman on the Hornchurch School Board; chairman of the local Bench of Magistrates; chairman of the Central Conservative Council for the Romford Division of Essex; and the first representative for the parish of Hornchurch on the Essex County Council. He was also Justice of the Peace for Romford. Holmes was involved with charities and good causes, and was widely acknowledged as being a benevolent man. He let his estate be used for various festivities and cricket matches were played there on a regular basis.

Langtons House, once the home of John Wagener.

Holmes established the First Essex Artillery Volunteers (No. 9 Hornchurch) in 1882. He became their captain, and rose to the status of colonel by the time the battery was disbanded in 1898. His son, Albert Arundel Holmes, was also involved in the unit and held the rank of captain.

There couldn't have been much spare time for recreation, but Colonel Holmes enjoyed hare coursing, and often entered his greyhounds for the Waterloo Cup. The three-day annual event was held on Lord Sefton's estate at Altcar, a few miles north of Liverpool. It was a knockout competition between sixty-four greyhounds, and was a major sporting event; it used to attract tens of thousands of spectators to watch and gamble on the coursing matches. To give an idea of how popular this event was, in the late 1800s carrier pigeons conveyed the results to major cities across the country and when news of the winner reached London, the Stock Exchange shut down for the rest of the day.

Colonel Holmes was eighty-five when he died on 3 December 1913, around six weeks after celebrating fifty years of marriage to Emilie. At the time of his death they had thirteen grandchildren. Shops and offices closed for the duration of the funeral, and local

Grey Towers, *c.* 1916. (Upminster Tithe Barn)

Col Holmes, Waterloo Cup event, 1908. (Upminster Tithe Barn)

Colonel Henry Holmes is buried in St Andrew's churchyard.

people lined the streets. It must have been quite a sight, as the horse-drawn carriage was followed by a procession of over seventy men from the fire brigade, the police service and the local Territorials. The Bishop of Barking took part in the service, which was held at St Andrew's Church. The church was packed with mourners, and the flag on the tower was lowered to half-mast, as were many flags around the village. Among the congregation were representatives from all the societies and organisations that he had been involved with. Sadly, just four months later Emilie Holmes also died – she was sixteen years younger than her husband.

Grey Towers became the headquarters of the First Sportsman's Battalion in November 1914. The battalion moved out in June 1915 and was replaced by the Pioneers' Battalion. However, it wasn't long before they moved on, and in 1916 New Zealand forces took their place. Eventually the building was used as a convalescent hospital for the New Zealanders, and from 1918 an educational programme was put in place to help servicemen get into employment after the war. All of the New Zealanders were evacuated from Grey Towers by 1919. In the post-war years it became a venue for scouts, girl guides and brownie camps. Grey Towers and its estate was bought by Mrs Elizabeth Parkes of Langtons in 1922. She sold it on to a developer in January 1929, and it was demolished in 1931. Now, the only reminders of this great estate are two streets: Grey Towers Gardens and Grey Towers Avenue.

Gymnasium for New Zealand troops. (Havering Libraries – Local Studies)

DID YOU KNOW?
There have been a number of sightings of ghosts at Bretons House in South Hornchurch. The building has a long history going back to the fifteenth century, but this does not account for the fact that on at two occasions Roman soldiers have been seen walking through walls in the basement by people who were working in there at the time. Someone else, who was working in the manor, heard a party going on in one of the rooms as he was walking up the stairs, but when he opened the door the room fell silent – no one was there.

6. The Hornchurch Connection

Over the years, Hornchurch has had its fair share of interesting characters either living in the area or associated with it. Some are famous, others infamous! Here are a few examples.

Susan Barker

The year was 1616 and Susan Barker, wife of Henry Barker from Upminster, was on trial at Chelmsford Assizes: she was accused of using witchcraft against three people living in Hornchurch. She was also accused of taking a scull from a grave with the intent of using it for witchcraft, charms and sorcery. She was acquitted on the charge of taking a scull and causing a woman named Mary Stephens to become 'consumed and mutilated'. However, she wasn't so lucky with the last two charges. She was accused of using witchcraft against Edward Ashen and his son (also Edward). They mysteriously became ill, growing weaker and weaker until they died. Edward Ashen (senior) was a blacksmith and was in his sixties. He had eight adult children and held offices in the parish of Hornchurch and the manor of Havering since mid-1590s. The year before his death he served as a constable.

Monument to Francis Rame in St Andrew's Church (1617).

William Stephens and Anne Stephens, who were witnesses in the trial, were related to Edward Ashen – which didn't bode well. On top of that, another witness was Francis Rame, a learned lawyer. In 1572 he was named Clerk of the Peace for Essex. Rame was also steward to Sir Anthony Cooke of Gidea Hall who was tutor to Edward VI – impressive credentials indeed. It's possible that without his testimony Susan may have been acquitted on these charges. She was found guilty of witchcraft and hanged. Francis Rame on the other hand has a monument in St Andrew's Church.

Thomas Witherings

Although English kings had maintained a royal post for official correspondence since 1516, letters for the public were not admitted. That changed on 31 July 1635 when Charles I authorised Thomas Witherings of Hornchurch, a member of the Mercers Company, to establish a public postal system.

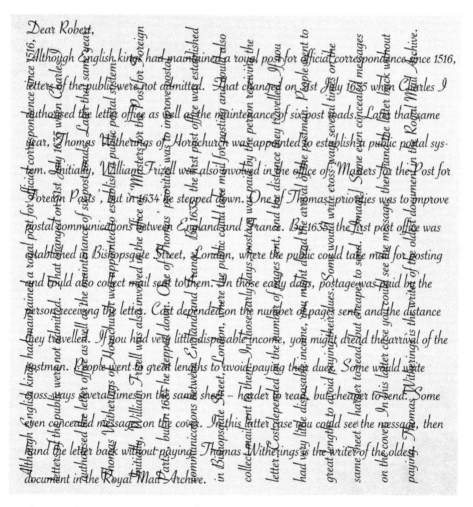

It wasn't unusual to write crossways on a letter.

Later that year, in October, the first post office was established in Bishopsgate Street, London, where the public could take mail for posting and could also collect mail sent to them. Thomas Witherings is the writer of the oldest document in the Royal Mail Archive; it was a letter dated 28 January 1636 to the Mayor of Hull, admonishing him for not punishing 'such delinquents who are continuing to use private mails'. Two post houses were also established in Barbican and Charing Cross in 1637. The king saw the new postal service as an opportunity, and surveillance was set up to look for any signs of dissent in the correspondence.

In the early days of the postal service, the recipient had to pay a fee calculated on both the number of sheets sent and the distance. For instance, a single sheet letter under 80 miles distance would cost 2*d* and a double sheet letter would cost 4*d*. If the sender lived more than 140 miles away, the cost would escalate to 6*d* for a single letter and 12*d* for a double letter. The value today of 12*d* (or a shilling), would be nearly £6. If you had very little disposable income, you might dread the arrival of the postman. People went to great lengths to avoid paying their dues. Some would write crossways several times on the same sheet – harder to read, but cheaper to send. Some even concealed messages on the cover. In this latter case the recipient could see the message, then hand the letter back without paying.

In April 1640, Witherings was elected Member of Parliament for Morpeth in Northumberland. He purchased the Nelmes Manor House in Hornchurch and lived there with his wife Dorothy and young son in 1646. However, in 1649 Witherings faced

Nelmes Manor House. (Havering Libraries – Local Studies)

a crisis that could ruin him. On 2 April, he was accused of assisting Lord Goring in the insurrection that had taken place in Essex in 1648, during the second phase of the English Civil War. Shortly afterwards, orders were issued to seize all of his money, goods and estate. In May he petitioned for the charge to be dropped, saying he had always faithfully served parliament. He took his plea to the County Commissioners, who unanimously agreed that there was no cause for taking legal possession of his assets. He was discharged, with no further proceedings against him.

Although greatly relieved by this, Witherings' health suffered, prompting him to make a will. On Sunday 28 September 1651 he collapsed and died on his way to a service at St Andrew's Church, where he was an elder. It is thought his death was caused by a stroke. There is a memorial to Thomas Witherings in the church, which also mentions his son, who died when he was five.

The Royal Mail is one of the oldest organisations in the world. Thomas Witherings is recognised as playing an important role in creating the postal system in Britain. His name even appears on the West 33rd Street façade of the post office building in New York, USA.

Monument to Thomas Witherings in St Andrew's Church (1651).

Augustine Garland

Born in 1603, Augustine Garland was the son of a London attorney. He was educated at Emmanuel College, Cambridge, and Lincoln's Inn, London. When his father died in 1637 he inherited an estate in South Hornchurch, which comprised Peacocks Farm, a house, two orchards and ten pasture fields. He was called to the Bar in January 1639 and was made Justice of the Peace for Essex in December 1645. Garland obviously moved around because it's known that in August 1644 he was residing at Great Ilford, Essex, and in June 1646 Garland was recorded as being a parishioner and resident at Barking, Essex. He had also inherited property in Kent and it was through this he was elected as an MP for Queenborough in 1648.

Following the end of the English Civil War, Augustine Garland became regicide (signatory of the king's death warrant), along with fifty-eight others, including Oliver Cromwell. Charles I was brought to trial in Westminster Hall on 20 January 1649, and the death sentence was proclaimed on 27 January.

When Charles II acceded the throne eleven years later, the surviving regicides that could be found were tried in the hall. It was not uncommon in Britain at the time to dig up your enemies after they had died to accuse them of wrong doings and punish them again! This posthumous execution happened to Oliver Cromwell and three others. Cromwell was removed from Westminster Abbey, put on trial and hung from the famous gallows at Tyburn. He then had his head chopped off and put on a spike on the roof of Westminster Hall, where it stayed for over twenty years.

Many of the remaining regicides fled the country or had died, a few were pardoned, and the others were either sent to prison or were transported. Nine were condemned and executed, four of which were hanged, drawn and quartered. Garland was sentenced to death, but this was commuted to life imprisonment. A warrant for his transportation to Tangier, Morocco, was issued in 1664, but it is not known whether this was ever carried out. At that time Tangier was under English occupation as it was part of the dowry for the princess Catherine of Portugal when she was betrothed to Charles II. There is a record showing that the estate Garland inherited in South Hornchurch was sold for £490 between 1664 and 1665.

Edward Nokes

Edward Nokes (1746–1802) lived in Hornchurch with his wife and children in abject poverty and filth. It is said that he fed his family on grains and offal, which he purchased at reduced prices. When any of his children died, Nokes would find a wooden box for their disposal. He never mourned them; in fact it was a case of out of sight out of mind. The family were probably pitied, but what neighbours didn't know (his wife included) was that Edward had a secret: he was a wealthy man. When he died it was discovered that he profited from property worth around £6,000 – the equivalent of hundreds of thousands of pounds in today's money.

It is said that he never washed his shirt, but after wearing it until it became black, he washed it in urine to save on the expense of soap. By trade he was a tinker and would have earned his living by mending things and selling everyday items, so how he came by his fortune is unknown.

Nokes used to keep money in a pot, which was hidden in a space in the kitchen wall behind a loose brick. One day his wife discovered the hoard and took a guinea. She was found out when her husband counted the coins. To the day of his death, even on his deathbed, he never spoke to her without adding 'thief' to every utterance. His death was no doubt hastened by his daily consumption of a quart of spirits. He didn't leave a will and his fortune was equally divided among his wife and surviving children. Apparently, his last request was that no nails were to be used in his coffin, because of the cost...

Bill Barazetti

Most people will have heard about Sir Nicholas Winton, the man who orchestrated the escape of around 700 Jewish children from Czechoslovakia to England at the beginning of the Second World War. However, other people who were involved with the Kindertransport may not be so well known. One of them, Bill Barazetti, ended up living in Mill Cottage, by the Dell in Hornchurch.

Born Werner Theodore Barazetti, he was the son of a Swiss professor. Back in 1938, he lived in German-occupied Prague with his wife Anna. In January 1939, Barazetti was recommended to Winton to work on the Kindertransports. His job was to organise trains, interview the families and send the children's details and photographs to London. He also arranged documents to be forged to ensure the safe passage of the children.

There is no doubt that Barazetti risked his life in the part he played. He finally came to England in August 1939 with his wife Anna and their son just before the start of the war in September. He was subsequently employed in a War Office unit, which interrogated captured German pilots. He become naturalised as a British citizen in 1953.

Bill Barazetti (right) receiving his certificate. (Yad Vashem)

Many years later, he became treasurer of the international writers' society, PEN. It wasn't until 1989, when he attended a PEN conference in Maastricht, that his story came to light. He struck up a conversation with an Israeli who spoke English with a pronounced German accent; it transpired that he had come to England on a Kindertransport from Berlin. Barazetti told him that he had played a small part in the Czechoslovakian operation. The Israeli passed this information on to another friend who tracked down Barazetti through the diaries that Winton had not long before passed over to the Holocaust conference organiser, Dr Elisabeth Maxwell. Finally, in 1993 the Jerusalem Holocaust Memorial Institute, Yad Vashem, honoured Barazetti as one of the Righteous among the Gentiles. Bill Barazetti lived in Mill Cottage until he died on 24 September 2000.

DID YOU KNOW?
Olympic medallist Mark Hunter MBE used to attend Havering Sixth Form College in Wingletye Lane. Mark won his gold medal in the lightweight double skulls rowing event at the Beijing Olympics in 2008 and a silver at London 2012. He gave an inspirational talk to the students at the sixth form college about reaching their true potential in 2013, when he retired from the sport. He is now a programme director at London Youth Rowing, a charity that works with 130 secondary schools across the capital to inspire youngsters to get into rowing.

7. Recreation

Through the centuries, the people of Hornchurch enjoyed various forms of recreation and entertainment. In medieval times, religious holidays provided the opportunity to attend festivals and local fairs. Wrestling, cockfighting and bear-baiting were popular, as were minstrels, acrobats, jugglers and troupes of actors in costume (mummers).

Archery contests were encouraged, as it was a skill needed for the defence of the land. In the 1100s, Henry I introduced a law to absolve any archer if he killed another while practising. In the reign of Edward III, a law was passed that stipulated the only form of sport allowed on Sundays and holidays was longbow practice. By the Tudor period, Henry VIII passed a law where men up to the age of sixty had to regularly practice archery at the 'butts' – these were usually mounds of earth in a field. It is widely assumed that Butts Green Road in Hornchurch is named after such a place.

The Dell, situated behind St Andrew's Church, was once a gravel pit. By the eighteenth century it was covered in grass. The banks formed a perfect amphitheatre for thousands of spectators watching events, such as wrestling and bare-knuckle fighting. The Mill Field next to the Dell also held sporting events.

MILL AND DELL, HORNCHURCH

The Mill Field leading to The Dell.

Hornchurch is one of the earliest pioneers of cricket in Essex, and early in the nineteenth century the Hornchurch Cricket Club was said to be outstanding. It was recorded in 1829: 'the Hornchurch players had not been beaten for seven years'.

The club was first established in 1783 when matches were played at Langtons Park. At this time wagers were made on the match and the winning side often received around a guinea for each player, but amounts varied. A match that took place on Monday 13 June 1785, between the gentlemen of Hornchurch and the gentlemen of Middlesex, was for 100 guineas. Local historian Charles Perfect said: 'Wagering continued to increase until the first quarter of the nineteenth century, when matches were often played for stakes of 500 to 1,000 guineas a side' – a fortune in those days.

A new Hornchurch club was formed in 1889 and played in Grey Towers Park. This continued until the First World War. Following on from that, a field was used in Wingletye Lane until 1925. The club was then offered a ground in front of Fairkytes, Billet Lane, now the Queen's Theatre. Eventually, the local council had plans to redevelop the area and in 1954 the Hornchurch Cricket Club took up the offer of a new pitch at Harrow Lodge Park, where they still play today.

A famous boxing match took place in Hornchurch in 1795. Daniel Mendoza, from Bethnal Green, was a well-known Jewish boxer. He was England's sixteenth Heavyweight Champion from 1792 to 1795, and is the first middleweight to ever win the Heavyweight Championship of the World. A match for the championship was arranged to take place in the Dell on 15 April 1795 between Mendoza and 'Gentleman' John Jackson.

Jackson was five years younger, 4 inches (10 cm) taller and 42 pounds (19 kg) heavier. However, Mendoza was the first boxer to develop a 'scientific style', which incorporated what he called 'side-stepping', moving around, ducking, blocking and avoiding punches. At the time, this was revolutionary.

A game of cricket being played at Harrow Lodge Park.

In those days, fights ended when an opponent was knocked out or unable to continue and could go on for a long time – records show some matches lasted for fifty rounds. However, on this occasion, the match only lasted just under eleven minutes. After a few rounds, Mendoza was bleeding badly from a terrible gash over his right eye. Jackson had no qualms in grabbing his opponent's long black hair in a tight grip in his left hand, while he continuously punched him in the face with his right hand. Mendoza was knocked unconscious – boxers tended to keep their hair short after this match. A few days later, the *Kentish Gazette* said: 'Among those who disgraced themselves by witnessing and consequently patronizing this exhibition, were the Duke of Hamilton, Colonel Hamilton, Sir Thomas Apreece, and Colonel Durant'.

After 1795 Mendoza began to seek other sources of income and became the landlord of the Admiral Nelson pub in Whitechapel. Interestingly, the actor Peter Sellers was Mendoza's great-great-grandson, and he hung portraits of the boxer in the backgrounds of several of his films. Sir Henry Cooper unveiled a commemorative plaque of Mendoza in 2008, which is displayed on the wall of Queen Mary University of London. Tower Hamlets have placed an English Heritage blue plaque on the building where Mendosa used to live in Bethnal Green. It says: 'Daniel Mendoza – Pugilist – 1764–1836. English Champion who proudly billed himself as 'Mendoza the Jew', lived here when writing "The Art of Boxing"'.

Daniel Mendoza plaque at Queen Mary University of London.

Daniel Mendoza lived in this house in Bethnal Green, London.

One tradition that lasted for centuries in Hornchurch was the annual Christmas Day wrestling match; the prize being a boar's head. Apparently it did lapse for a while, but was reinstated in 1824. There is a report in the *Essex Herald* on 3 January 1837 that said the match had taken place on 26 December as Christmas Day was a Sunday. It describes the scene as picturesque, as the country was whitened with snow:

> The spectators formed a large ring, on the margin of which, held by the senior workman upon a high pole, was the boar's head, tastefully decorated with holly and light blue ribbons, a lemon being placed beneath his ample tusks.

Ten contestants entered the ring and when the winner was declared the prize was paraded around the village before being feasted upon in one of the inns. The contest usually took place in the Mill Field, next to the Dell. It last took place in 1868, when local residents petitioned for it to be stopped after a match between the men of Hornchurch and the men of Romford developed into a rowdy affair.

A pleasure fair was traditionally held on Whit Monday in High Street until 1878, when it was abolished by statutory order because it had become a nuisance.

The first cinema to open in Hornchurch was situated in Station Lane (on the site of the present Ripon House development). The Hornchurch Cinema Company Ltd opened

Towers Cinema, *c*. 1935.

The name is the only link to the art deco building.

its doors on 18 December 1913. To begin with, the building was packed most nights. At that time, silent, black and white films were shown, brought to life by the pianist conveying the drama, or humour, flickering on the screen. No doubt the First World War had quite an effect on business because by 1915 the cinema was in serious financial trouble, and by 1917 the debts had grown so large that a receiver was appointed. The company was dissolved in October 1919. However, by 1920 the Hornchurch Cinema reopened. Unfortunately, no records can be traced to give any further information about the cinema, except that it closed in 1934. It is thought that the building was used in the war years as a depot for medical supplies and later for the storage of furniture from bombed buildings.

The Towers Cinema, in High Street, Hornchurch, was a far superior property. It was built on part of the Grey Towers' site after its demolition in 1931. The *Chelmsford Chronicle* was glowing in its report published on 9 August 1935, on the eve of its formal opening:

> The new cinema is the last word in elegance and comfort. Having seating accommodation for 2,000, a special system of air purification, perfect acoustic properties, ballroom, cafe, and car park for 1,000 cars, it represents a triumph of constructional skill.

In 1939, The Towers was taken over by Eastern Cinemas, and again in 1943 by Oscar Deutsch's Odeon Theatres. Financially, it seemed to be doing all right. On Sunday 28 May 1950, thieves used explosives to blow open the safe, getting away with around £300 (equivalent to around £10,000 today). It was renamed Odeon from 1950 and closed in 1973 when it became a bingo hall. The iconic art deco building was demolished in 2017, despite residents' vigorous efforts to protect it from being destroyed. A Lidl supermarket now stands in its place.

The Hornchurch Urban District Council bought the dilapidated cinema building in Station Lane in 1948, and after much discussion it was eventually decided to renovate it and open it up as a theatre. On Monday 21 September 1953, the coronation year, Sir Ralph Richardson opened the Queen's Theatre, which seated 379 people. By 1955 the theatre was producing up to twenty-five plays a year. A number of well-known figures in theatre and television once appeared at the Queen's, including Nigel Hawthorne, Prunela Scales, Philip Madoc, Bernard Cribbens, Leslie Phillips and Wilfred Bramble.

The theatre proved to be very popular, although audiences did decline as time went on. However, the London Borough of Havering had faith that a new, larger theatre would be well received. So, in 1973 building work began on the site of the old cricket pitch opposite Fairkytes.

The last show to be performed at the theatre in Station Lane was the pantomime *Sleeping Beauty*, which took place on Saturday 8 February 1975. However, theatregoers didn't have too long to wait for the next production to take place. On Wednesday 2 April 1975, Sir Peter Hall opened the Queen's Theatre in Billet Lane. Its first show was a rock musical: *Joseph and the Amazing Technicolour Dreamcoat*. The new theatre had the capacity to seat around 500 people.

Since then the theatre, which is a registered charity, has survived many financial cutbacks. Elizabeth II and Prince Philip paid a visit on its fiftieth anniversary in 2003,

Queen's Theatre, Station Lane, in the 1960s. (Queen's Theatre Archive)

Queen's Theatre, Billet Lane, 2019.

The Queen listening to Corrigan's Band of Hope, 2003. (© Christine Sutton)

Acker Bilk at the Queen's Theatre in 1986. (© Christine Sutton)

and the theatre celebrated its diamond jubilee in 2013. Besides entertaining over 200,000 people each year, the theatre is involved with educational programmes, youth theatre groups, activities for children, workshops and classes. It is also a winner of UK Theatre's Most Welcoming Theatre 2016 and 2017.

DID YOU KNOW?
In October 1938, Hornchurch Council debated whether the Towers Cinema should be allowed to open on Sundays. Revd E. W. Grevatt, vicar of All Saints Church, said they had to prevent the deterioration of Sunday: 'There was too much blatant pleasure, Sunday having become a first-class bank holiday'. The idea was rejected. Ratepayers complained and were allowed their own poll some weeks later; the majority were in favour. In February 1939, the Home Secretary approved Sunday opening for cinemas in Hornchurch, Essex, and High Wycombe, Buckinghamshire.

8. The War Years

During the First World War, the War Ministry requisitioned Suttons Farm, Hornchurch, for military use; London was only 15 miles away flying in a straight line so it was an ideal location. The farm, run by Tom Crawford, covered an area of around 90 acres. At the time it was still owned by New College, Oxford.

On Sunday 3 October 1915, the Royal Flying Corps (RFC) Station Suttons Farm was established. To begin with there were just two pilots who flew BE2c biplanes, and a small number of ground crew; some of the men were billeted in the farmhouse and others in the local White Hart public house while the site was made ready.

The threat to London was the German airships – the dreaded Zeppelins – which were a type of rigid airship named after the German Count Ferdinand von Zeppelin. The name was commonly used for many different types of airships, including those built by Luftschiffbau Shütte-Lanz in 1916, which were less flammable. They employed machine guns for defence and carried a varying bomb load, usually 2 tons or more. They were capable of changing direction relatively quickly without changing speed. Coupled with their low fuel consumption, which allowed them to be in the air for long periods of time, they proved to be a difficult target for the RFC. The airships would fly at night to avoid being hit by artillery. Even if they were caught in the beams of the searchlights it wasn't easy to bring them down as they could increase their altitude quite quickly and hide in the clouds. They were also very quiet.

The BE2c biplanes used by the RFC had 90-horse-power engines and struggled to attain a speed of 82 mph. It could take between forty and fifty minutes to climb to the operating height of the airships, at around 10,000 feet. They had a small fuel capacity, so reconnaissance missions only used to last for a couple of hours. On top of that they had open cockpits and very few instruments on board. The planes were armed with small bombs, and the pilots had grenades and a machine gun with special incendiary bullets that could penetrate the outer envelope of the airship and explode inside the structure.

Reluctant Hero

Since the base opened at Suttons Farm, pilots had encountered a number of Zeppelins but, like other RFC stations, had not been able to destroy one in the air. By April 1916 the number of pilots and aircraft had grown to six at Hornchurch, and formed part of 39 Home Defence Squadron, which had its headquarters at Hounslow. On 2 September 1916, the Germans launched the heaviest raid of the war and sent sixteen airships to target London.

Lieutenant William Leefe Robinson, who was twenty-one at the time, set off from Suttons Farm on his mission to patrol the Thames shortly after 2300 hours. Two hours later he spied an airship over Woolwich; unfortunately, by the time he got nearer it had

LIEUT. WILLIAM LEEFE ROBINSON, V.C.,
Worcester Regiment and R.F.C.,
Who brought down the Zeppelin at Cuffley, near Enfield.
ST. JAMES' PRESS, ROSOMAN ST., CLERKENWELL, E.C.

Lt William Leefe
Robinson VC (1916).

climbed higher and was lost in the clouds. Then he caught sight of one illuminated by searchlights in the distance – it had been dropping bombs over Edmonton and Enfield. It was now just before 0200 hours and Robinson made the decision to intercept, even though he should have been flying back to base by then.

After firing at the airship from different angles without any affect, he got behind it and concentrated his fire on one spot at the rear of the structure, and that did the trick. He was euphoric as he watched the airship dissolve into flames and crash to the ground; the wreckage landed at Cuffley, Hertfordshire. Over the coming days and weeks it is estimated that 10,000 people went by train from King's Cross to see what was left of the SL-11. The funeral of the airship crew took place at Potter Bar on 6 September 1916.

Wreckage of the SL-11 airship at Cuffley.

The funeral of the Cuffley Zeppelin's crew: R.F.C. officers bearing the coffin of the commander.

[Photopress.

The funeral of the airship crew. (Hornchurch Aerodrome Historical Trust)

Leefe Robinson's public destruction of the German airship lifted the spirit of the nation, making him a national hero. Besides being the first person to shoot down an airship over mainland Britain, he had done so on low fuel tanks and very little oil, barely getting back to base in one piece. At the end of his report to his commanding officer, he said:

> On landing I found I had shot away the machine gun wire guard, the rear part of the centre section and had pierced the rear main spar several times.

Within forty-eight hours, it was announced that he would be awarded the Victoria Cross (the fastest ever recorded). He was also promoted to captain. In the three months afterwards, five more airships were shot down using his combat technique. A publicity photo was released in October 1916 showing Leefe Robinson, Wulstan Tempest and Frederick Sowrey as the Zeppelin wreckers.

His actions boosted the morale of Londoners and they were keen to show their appreciation. For thousands of people it was without doubt one of the most memorable events of the entire war. Wherever he went crowds mobbed him – his photo was in newspapers and magazines everywhere. Captain Leefe Robinson was awarded £3,500 in prize money by well-wishers (pilots earned around a pound a day at the time), and a silver cup donated by the people of Hornchurch. He bought a new Prince Henry Vauxhall car with some of the money.

However, he wasn't comfortable with his new fame, so he asked to go on active service in France. During his first patrol on 5 April 1917, he encountered a formation of six aircraft led by Manfred von Richthofen 'the Red Baron'. Sebastian Festner shot him down

Zeppelin wreckers: Robinson, Tempest and Sowrey. (Hornchurch Aerodrome Historical Trust)

in a dogfight. He was taken prisoner and was held in a number of camps throughout the rest of the war. As the famous 'Zeppelin destroyer', he spent months in solitary confinement and was generally badly treated. Even though he wasn't in the best of health, he made several attempts to escape. He survived the war but succumbed to the flu virus that had killed millions. Captain William Leefe Robinson VC died on 31 December 1918 at Stanmore, aged just twenty-three.

By the time the war drew to a close, the Royal Flying Corps had become the Royal Air Force, and RAF Hornchurch had 300 airmen and twenty-four WRAFs (later known as Women's Auxiliary Air Force – WAAFs). Towards the end of 1919, it was decided to decommission the aerodrome. Life returned to normal and Tom Crawford got his farm back. He was to enjoy four years of farming before the government stepped in again – this time they had a compulsory purchase order.

RAF Suttons Farm

The government bought 120 acres of farmland from New College in 1923 as part of its new Home Defence Force. It took four years to get RAF Suttons Farm in full operational order. By the time the Second World War broke out in 1939, there were sixty Spitfire pilots based at the airfield.

RAF Hornchurch was ideally located to protect both London and the Thames corridor from German air attacks. This also made the aerodrome a target for the Luftwaffe; over the course of the Second World War it was bombed on twenty occasions. The airfield defended itself with anti-aircraft guns and crew positioned in Tett Turrets. Bombing

RAF Hornchurch. (With permission of aviation artist Barry Weekley)

The squadrons making up the Hornchurch Wing. (Upminster Tithe Barn)

missions were never that accurate, so Hornchurch and the surrounding areas often suffered casualties and heavy damage to housing.

During its life as an RAF base, Hornchurch became home to many squadrons, becoming the most renowned Spitfire station in fighter command. Walter Bygraves, known as Max Bygraves, singer and entertainer, was one of the men who maintained the Spitfires. He met Blossom Murray, who was a WAAF at Hornchurch in 1941, and married her the following year.

One pilot who was highly respected at the time was Brendan Eamon Fergus 'Paddy' Finucane DSO DFC and Two Bars. He was the RAF's youngest ever Wing Commander at twenty-one, and one of its most decorated Spitfire Aces. He was appointed to lead the 'Hornchurch Wing' in 1942. On 15 July that year, he led the wing in a fighter 'Ramrod' ground attack operation, targeting a German Army camp at Étaples France, German shipping at Ostend, and strafing three airfields. Finucane's wing then regrouped to return to Hornchurch, but as the group passed at low level over the beach at Pointe Du Touquet, his Spitfire was hit by machine gun fire that severely damaged his radiator. The engine overheated and his Spitfire began losing altitude, which meant Finucane was too low to bail out. His last words were 'This is it, chaps'.

Officers outside the mess in 1940. (Hornchurch Aerodrome Historical Trust)

Spitfire damaged at RAF Hornchurch, August 1940. (Purfleet Heritage Centre)

222 Squadron groundcrew on a Spitfire, 1940. (Purfleet Heritage Centre)

It was reported by witnesses that after a near-perfect 'splash landing' the Spitfire sank like a stone and despite all efforts Finucane was never seen again. At the time of his death, Finucane's score stood at an amazing thirty-two victories. He would have been twenty-two years old on 16 October 1942.

The locals would have considered all of the pilots heroes. Some would gain international recognition. Squadron Leader Roger Bushell, Flying Officer William Ash and Wing Commander Joseph Kayll played a crucial role in the 'great escape' from Stalag Luft III in 1944. They had all been shot down and captured in France after taking off from RAF Hornchurch on various missions.

In 1943, Roger Bushell (codename Big X) created an escape committee – Joseph Kayll took on the role of head of intelligence. The plan was to help 200 Allied prisoners escape via three tunnels named Tom, Dick and Harry. Bushell was the basis for the character 'Roger Bartlett', played by Richard Attenborough, in the film called *The Great Escape*. They based Steve McQueen's character, Virgil Hilts, on William Ash (cooler king) from Texas. However, in real life, Ash was in the 'cooler' at the time of the escape on 24 March 1944. Seventy-six men escaped, all but three were recaptured. Fifty of those prisoners, including Bushell, were shot by the Gestapo on Hitler's order. Joseph Kayll and William Ash survived the war and lived to a ripe old age.

Second World War pillbox.

RAF Hornchurch lost its Fighter Command status in June 1945 and was transferred to Technical Training Command. It became the selection centre for aircrew. Comedian Ronnie Corbett did his national service with the RAF and became a pilot officer. In the early 1950s he was based at Hornchurch. He was acknowledged as the shortest commissioned officer in the British Armed Forces. One of the applicants to pass through the centre in 1949 was Aircraftman Second Class Norman Tebbit, who later in his life became an MP, cabinet minister and then a lord.

The Legacy

The Air Ministry sold two-thirds of the airfield to the Hoveringham Gravel Company in 1963. They excavated gravel for the best part of a decade before the quarry was used as a refuse tip. Most of the former administrative and technical areas, including the two Type A and one Type C hangars, were levelled in the 1960s to create a new housing development. It is known locally as the Airfield Estate and many of the roads bear the names of pilots, airfields or aircraft.

In 1980, the London Borough of Havering carried out large-scale landscaping and created Hornchurch County Park. Various structures of the site's RAF history, such as pillboxes, the Blenheim dispersal pen and gun emplacements, together with the largest number of surviving Tett Turrets in England, are still visible within the park.

Hornchurch has the largest number of surviving Tett turrets in England.

A stone circle indicates the site of a gun emplacement.

This image was shared around the world. (© Martin Le-May)

This dispersal hut from the airfield was put to good use.

The headstone of Raimund Sanders Draper in St Andrew's churchyard.

The remembrance garden dedicated to Second World War allied forces.

Around 150,000 visitors a year visit the park, which is part of the Ingrebourne Valley nature reserve. In March 2015 it was part of a national news item. Amateur photographer Martin Le-May was walking over the park with his wife Ann, when he heard a distressed squawking noise. He couldn't believe his eyes when he saw a weasel attacking a green woodpecker, which had jumped on the bird's back. Martin managed to catch the extraordinary moment with his camera when the woodpecker took off with the weasel tightly hanging on. When he put the photo on social media he was astounded by the reaction – the image went viral and was retweeted thousands of times. It was picked up by a number of news channels around the world, including the BBC.

To the west of the park, some of the administrative and accommodation buildings from the airfield can still be found. These include the officers' mess (Astra House), officers' quarters (Astra Close, West, North and East) and women officers' quarters (Nos 89-99 Wood Lane, odd numbers). A dispersal hut, which would have been used by pilots waiting to scramble on a moment's notice, was relocated to Woodhall Crescent in the 1980s, and is now used by the Havering Association for people with disabilities (HAD).

R. J. Mitchell School was named after the designer of the Supermarine Spitfire, and Sanders School was named after an American pilot, Flying Officer Raimund Sanders Draper. It is believed that he sacrificed his life on 24 March 1943 to prevent his Spitfire hitting, what was at the time, Suttons School. His aircraft developed engine trouble after taking off and bystanders believe that he intended passing to the left of the school in an attempt to land on the open ground beyond. Realising that with reduced power he could possibly hit the school, he deliberately put the nose of the Spitfire down in the playing field. He died on impact, aged twenty-nine.

The RAF Hornchurch Heritage Centre.

Although there is a small display space in the Ingrebourne Valley Visitor Centre, in the Hornchurch Country Park, the Hornchurch Aerodrome Historical Trust wanted a permanent home for all of the artefacts, photographs and personal stories relating to the history of the airfield. The opportunity came when the construction company Bellway Homes, who had purchased the former site of St George's Hospital, gifted Suttons House to them in 2018. It was formerly two staff cottages for Suttons Institute from 1938, and then used by RAF Hornchurch from 1939 until 1946. It became part of St George's Hospital in 1948, and then finally used by NELFT North East London NHS Foundation Trust until its closure. The RAF Hornchurch Heritage Centre is due to open in early 2020.

DID YOU KNOW?
Archaelogists Tony Pollard and Neil Oliver took part in the BBC programme *Two Men in a Trench* in 2004, which looked at the role RAF Hornchurch played in the Battle of Britain. They uncovered some interesting objects, including a pair of 1940 RAF pilot's goggles, oddments such as an RAF eggcup and assorted items from a first aid kit. They excavated an E type dispersal pen, a Tett turret and a gun emplacement on the northern end of the site. A partially buried pillbox was also excavated.

9. Children of the Parish

In the Tudor period, children aged between five and seven received basic learning at petty or dame schools. Normally the lessons took place either in local homes or in some villages at the local church hall. However, many did not go to school at all, as parents had to contribute to the cost of their child's education. It wasn't unknown for poor boys, as young as seven or eight, to be apprenticed to learn a trade.

Charity Schools

The first charity school for the poor of Hornchurch, Romford and Havering was founded in 1710 and was situated in Romford. To begin with lessons were taught in two houses, but by 1728 St Edward's charity school was relocated to the top end of the market. In the early days it had around forty boys and twenty girls, and funding came from donations and subscriptions from benefactors. Children were clothed by the school and instructed in the fundamental principles of the Christian religion. Boys were taught reading, writing and arithmetic; they were also placed as apprentices. Girls were instructed in reading, writing, sewing and knitting. They received four years' education, and were admitted from the age of eight to twelve. When they left school they were provided with bibles and prayer books. By 1813 the number of children attending had risen to ninety, but this was still a very small number of pupils as Hornchurch, Romford and Havering had a population of more than 6,000. However, it wasn't until 1834 that the governors of the school decided that they needed to expand the premises so they could take in more children. The plan was to erect a large schoolroom for the boys and to give the old one to the girls. They also decided to establish an infant school. One of the governors said: 'At each half-yearly meeting a crowd of poor little applicants are consequently rejected, consigned to the streets, to ignorance and ruin. Thank heaven, their rescue is at hand!' By 1840 just over 200 children were 'saved from ignorance and idleness'. The school building lasted until 1926, when it was sold to Essex County Council. They turned it into a public library in 1930. Other premises were found, but by the mid-1960s the primary and secondary classes separated to create the two schools that we know today: St Edward's Church of England Primary School and St Edward's Church of England Academy.

Aylett's School was founded in 1731. When Alice Aylett died she left land in a trust to pay £10 yearly to a schoolmaster, appointed by the parish, to teach ten poor boys. Aylett's School didn't have a building, so children were taught in the church vestry. The first schoolmaster was appointed in 1746. When William Jacobs died in 1813 he left £200 in trust to Aylett's School. By 1837 ten poor boys were being taught reading, writing and arithmetic along with several paying pupils in the master's house. The school ceased to exist by 1856, but in 1890 the Charity Commission scheme required the income from Aylett's and Jacobs' charities to be used for prizes for Hornchurch children.

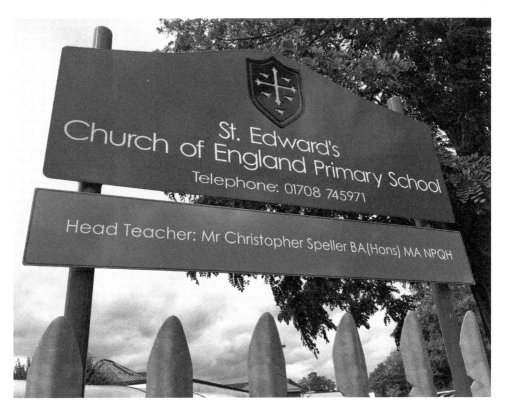

St Edward's Primary School's history dates from the eighteenth century.

A school was built on charity land belonging to the Skeale's family, in South End Road, South Hornchurch, in 1864. It was funded by the income of the Skeale's charity, subscriptions and savings from national school funds. Sixty-three children were being taught there by 1871. The school received annual government grants from 1885. The school board took it over in 1890 and was replaced by South Hornchurch board school in 1899.

Free Education

A national school system was developed in the 1800s by the National Society for Promoting Religious Education. Their aim was: 'the national religion should be made the foundation of national education, and should be the first and chief thing taught to the poor, according to the excellent liturgy and catechism provided by our Church'.

In 1844, a national school was built close to the Chaplaincy, which was used as a church building in later years. New College, Oxford, gave land for a new school for girls and infants to be built in North Street in 1855, together with a house for the teacher. It is believed that the boys being taught at Aylett's School transferred to the national school in 1856. The area was developed further in 1874 when the boys were moved to a new school building, next to the teacher's house. Infants were transferred to the old building, sited near the Chaplaincy.

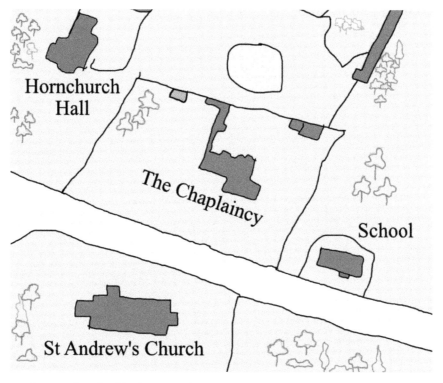

Diagram showing the school built next to the Chaplaincy.

These buildings in North Street were once part of a school.

Langtons Junior School in Westlands Avenue.

The Elementary Education Act of 1870 made provision for free elementary education of all children aged from five to thirteen years, and established school boards to oversee and complete the network of schools, bringing them all under some form of supervision. The national school received annual government grants from 1871. The school board took it over in 1889.

The population of Hornchurch was steadily growing, and by 1902 a new school opened in Westland Avenue – around 400 boys and girls attended. At the end of February in 1907 the school was closed for two weeks because of an outbreak of scarlet fever and diphtheria. The infants still used the 1855 buildings in North Street, but in 1926 new classrooms were built. The school was developed further in 1932 and reorganised in 1935 to cater for the juniors and infants.

Hornchurch Cottage Homes

The population of Hornchurch grew by over 300 children in 1889, when the Cottage Homes were opened to accommodate destitute children and orphans from Kingsland Road and Hoxton Workhouses in London. The poor-law guardians of the parish of St Leonard, Shoreditch, had approved the venture two years earlier when 80 acres of land,

The layout of the Cottage Homes, *c.* 1900. (Upminster Tithe Barn)

which was part of the Harrow Lodge estate, was purchased for £6,300. Eleven homes were built at a cost of £48,340, and each one had the capacity to take thirty children. There were five girls' and six boys' homes facing each other across a wide gravelled roadway that ran south from the entrance on Hornchurch Road. Two more cottages were added later on for the isolation of sick children.

The complex, which resembled a village, included a porter's lodge, superintendent's house, chapel, guardians' committee room, a probationary ward, schools for boys, girls and infants, playground, band room, stores, bakery, swimming bath, workshops, needle room, laundries, receiving room and infirmary. Each house had foster parents to look after the children. The rest of the land was rented out for farming.

Boys at the school were given a wide variety of industrial training including engineering, carpentry, painting, tailoring and shoemaking. Girls received training in a variety of domestic tasks. Some children would have been selected to migrate to the colonies, Canada being the most popular. This also applied to children in workhouses. Some of these children still had a parent alive, but they weren't consulted. Also, siblings may have travelled together but it was unlikely that they would have remained as a family unit. Life would have been harsh for the majority of these children. The boys would most likely end up working very long hours on farms and the girls put into domestic service. In April 1909, thirty-three boys and girls from the Cottage Homes, Hornchurch, appeared before Romford magistrates to obtain sanction to emigrate to Canada. Sending pauper children to the colonies was nothing new. Up to 150,000 British children were evacuated through government-approved schemes across 350 years from all around Britain. The

The Infants' Cottage, *c.* 1900. (Upminster Tithe Barn)

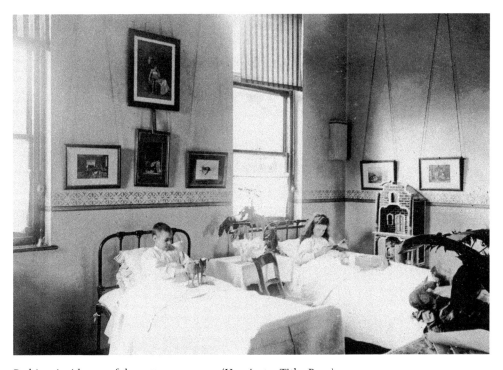

Bedtime inside one of the cottages, *c.* 1900. (Upminster Tithe Barn)

peak was between 1870 and 1920, when as many as 80,000 children were dispatched to Canada alone.

Over the years, the Cottage Homes received a number of high-profile visitors including bishops, cabinet ministers and Members of Parliament, but one of the most memorable visitors must have been Lieutenant William Leefe Robinson. He paid a visit shortly after he famously shot down the German airship over Cuffley, Hertfordshire, in September 1916. The children were extremely excited and presented him with a solid-silver, inscribed inkstand.

There was a change in the administration of the Cottage Homes in 1930 when the London County Council took over. It was transferred again in 1965 to the London Borough of Tower Hamlets; at this time it was known as St Leonard's Children's Home. Finally in 1984 they closed the home and sold the site for the development of 250 homes.

Private Schools

A number of small private schools sprang up in Hornchurch in the twentieth century. Between 1906 and 1937 ten private schools were listed in directories, but most of them were short-lived. Mrs Elizabeth Barnard advertised her school 'Cosy Cotte' in local papers in 1904, referring to herself as the principal and certified teacher of many years' experience. It was situated in Ernest Road, presumably in her house, and appears in *Kelly's Directory* in 1912. Likewise, Miss Gertrude Charles advertised her establishment, situated at Beethoven House, Butts Green Road, in the 1914 edition of *Kelly's Directory*.

Mrs Constance Murphy opened a kindergarten school at No. 56 Butts Green Road in 1932. Initially, she couldn't find a suitable school for her son John, so as she was a qualified teacher she decided to educate him at home. Her nephew Michael Adie, who used to live in Sylvan Avenue, joined him the next year when he was four. Both boys moved on to another school when aged around seven. Friends were keen to have their children taught by Mrs Murphy and by the Second World War she was teaching between six to eight children. She closed her school during the war years and reopened in 1945. After her husband died in 1950 she decided to expand, and at one time had forty-five pupils.

No. 56 Butts Green Road is now used as a nursery.

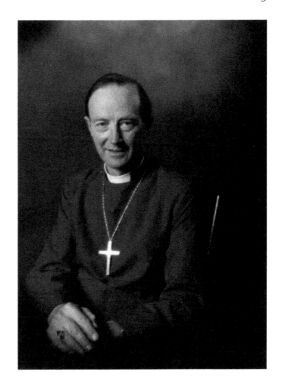

Michael Adie when he was Bishop of
Guildford. (© Michael Adie)

A classroom was built in the garden in 1954, and another added to the side of the house. Her daughter, Mrs Margaret Bearcroft, joined her in 1962 and dealt with the administrative side of things. Mrs Murphy continued teaching until four weeks before she died at the age of eighty-nine. Currently the building is used for a children's nursery.

Mrs Murphy's son went on to be a director of an advertising agency and his cousin Michael became Bishop of Guildford in 1983 until his retirement in 1994. He played a significant role in the General Synod that led to the ordination of women priests. He was chairman of the General Synod Board of Education and was awarded a CBE in the 1994 Birthday Honours for services to education. Michael has fond memories of his time with his aunt: 'She was an inspiring enthusiast, and when there was a break in the class work she took the children out to the tennis court for deep-breathing exercises. There was continuous action and considerable educational success'.

DID YOU KNOW?
In 1601, the Overseers of the Poor were given the ability to bind pauper children to a master; anyone under the age of twenty-one refusing to be an apprentice was to be imprisoned until they found a master. Originally, boys had to be aged from ten to eighteen years old to begin an apprenticeship, although the Parish Apprentices Act of 1698 reduced the allowable age of entry to seven.

10. The Growing Suburb of Hornchurch

It has taken many thousands of years to shape the area that is known today as Hornchurch. As we saw at the beginning of the story, the Anglian ice sheet made quite an impact, but it's the last 350 years that brought about its most dramatic development.

Transport

It is important for any growing community to have good transport links. For Hornchurch, besides the horse and wagon, the stagecoach would have brought people to and from the area in the eighteenth century. The coaching era is generally thought to have begun around 1660 and lasted until the late 1840s when the last passenger-carrying mail coaches and stage services were discontinued. In 1769 a stagecoach ran through Hornchurch to London five days a week. There was still only one coach a day in 1838. Many other coaches could be boarded at Romford. The fare worked out at roughly one shilling per mile, but the cost to the individual depended on how many shared the stagecoach – similar to a taxi. Even in those days there were people who tried to dodge paying their fare. A case was held at the Essex assizes in March 1803, concerning a passenger arriving at his destination in Hornchurch and not paying his fare. As he left the stagecoach to go into the inn he told the coachman not to follow him, otherwise he would 'poke his eye out'. The coachman, however, did follow him and asked for his fare; his reward was a stick thrust into his eye. The poor man fell down 'in a paroxysm of agony and anguish'.

The development of steam locomotives and railways in the 1830s certainly contributed to the end of stagecoaches and mail coaches. The London, Tilbury & Southend Railway opened a new line on 1 May 1885 that ran through the newly built Hornchurch station. They also constructed the Upminster to Romford branch line in 1892. Emerson Park station opened in 1909, which would have been a big incentive to further develop housing in the area. Hornchurch station was completely rebuilt in 1932 by the London, Midland & Scottish Railway, and two new platforms were constructed to serve the electric District Railway local service, which was extended from Barking to Upminster.

The London General Omnibus Company (LGOC) was founded in 1885 to amalgamate and regulate the many independent horse-drawn omnibus services then operating in London. By 1902 they began using motor omnibuses. In September 1912, the LGOC was petitioned to run a motor-bus service to Hornchurch, to link up with its Romford service. Hornchurch Bus Garage was opened in 1924 by the LGOC under the name 'Romford' – it cost £18,000 to build. It was renamed in 1953 when a new garage opened in North Street, Romford. Rebuilt in 1954, Hornchurch Garage was among the first to close in September 1988, as a result of route losses under competitive tendering.

Station Lane, *c.* 1905. It was known as Lake Street in the thirteenth to fifteenth centuries.

London, Tilbury and Southend Railway

OPENING OF THE NEW LINE

TO

DAGENHAM, HORNCHURCH AND UPMINSTER

THIS LINE WILL BE OPENED FOR TRAFFIC ON

1ST MAY 1885

FOR TRAIN SERVICES AND FURTHER PARTICULARS
SEE TIME TABLES

FARES FROM OR TO FENCHURCH STREET

	Single	1st	2nd	3rd	Return		
DAGENHAM ...		1/4	1/1	-/9	2/4	1/9	1/3
HORNCHURCH ...		1/6½	1/3	-/10½	2/9	2/1	1/6½
UPMINSTER ...		1/8	1/4	-/11	3/0	2/3	1/7

First, Second and Third Class will be conveyed by all trains

Fenchurch Street Terminus. April 1885 – BY ORDER

Newspaper notice advertising the new train service.

Hornchurch Bus Garage shortly after it closed. (Upminster Tithe Barn)

Fire Brigade

The first fire engine bought by Hornchurch parish vestry was in 1830. Mr Burchett Whennell offered to provide a fire engine 'for the preservation of property in case of accidents by fire' – it cost £18 10s 0d. A resolution was passed to keep the engine at the Poor House until a suitable building was erected. It's not known how long it was there but there are several references of the fire engine being housed at Hornchurch Brewery, High Street. The first horses to pull the manual pump were provided by the licensee of the Bull Inn. In 1894 the Hornchurch vestry was abolished and replaced by Hornchurch Parish Council. They removed the old manual engine from the brewery to the old Drill Hall, Billet Lane. By 1898 a uniformed voluntary fire brigade was formed, and two years later a new fire engine was purchased. An early call out method included a youngster on a bicycle blowing a bugle at strategic points in the village.

The first fire chief was Mr J. Wood. A few years later Mr Edgar G. Bratchell took over as captain and held the post for nearly thirty years. It is recorded that in 1901 the Hornchurch Fire Brigade tendered their resignations owing to 'unpleasantness over the use of the new engine in pumping out a well'. Explanations were offered to the parish council, and Captain Bratchell was commended. A vote of thanks was passed to the brigade for its past services, and they were asked to reconsider their resignations, which they did.

Colonel Henry Holmes donated land to the council so that a new fire station could be built in Billet Lane (now the site of Sainsbury's car park). At the opening ceremony on

Captain Bratchell holding a child's hand, *c.* 1907. (Havering Libraries – Local Studies)

The funeral procession of Edgar G. Bratchell. (Havering Libraries – Local Studies)

4 July 1907, Captain Bratchell arranged a short display for the parish council. Bratchell died in Oldchurch Hospital in April 1934, eight years after he left the fire service.

The brigade was eventually taken over by Hornchurch Urban District Council, and from 1936 it was operated on a full-time basis. Essex County Council, which took over the brigade after the Second World War, built a new station in North Street in 1963, where it still stands today.

Policing

From the sixteenth century, the court leet appointed petty constables for a period of one year. The post was unpaid and carried out in addition to the person's usual day job. They were typically local tradesmen or farmers, which meant that communities were 'policing' themselves. John Bayly was appointed as high constable for Hornchurch in April 1730 and John Badgee as petty constable. John Swallow was to cover north Hornchurch, and Thomas Saggett covered South Hornchurch.

Prisoners were taken to the village lock-up known as the 'cage' for temporary detention. It was very small, holding just two or three persons, and was situated in Cage Row – now North Street – and had been in use from the seventeenth century. Prisoners would usually be held overnight before being taken to the nearest jail.

Cage Row (now North Street), *c.* 1956. (Upminster Tithe Barn)

An order was given by the Romford Court Leet in January 1732 requesting the Hornchurch stocks, cage and watch house be repaired and that the constable should pay for the work to be carried out, for which he could then claim for his expenses.

The idea of professional policing was taken up by Sir Robert Peel when he became Home Secretary in 1822. In 1841 two constables were posted to Hornchurch. Over a number of years, constables came and went. They normally lived in or near to the village. It wasn't until 1931 that there was a police station in Hornchurch. A small terraced house in the High Street was purchased for a sergeant and constable to live in, which also acted as the police station. In 1955 the Essex Constabulary built a police station in Station Lane, which is now part of Havering Division of the Metropolitan Police.

Water Supply and Sewerage

Throughout the centuries the people of Hornchurch would have obtained their water from a local standpipe, well, stream or river. There were three wells serving the village: Soane's well in Suttons Lane; Mason's well, not far from St Andrew's Church, at the back of the windmill; and a well in a High Street orchard. Many paid for water to be delivered in a bucket. The modern era began with the South Essex Water Company in 1861. An official report from 1901 noted that the growing suburb of Hornchurch was entirely supplied by the company. However, Upminster's Hall Lane, Wingletye Lane in Hornchurch and Straight Road, Romford, had no mains for quite some time. As late as 1917, lack of water meant there was no fire brigade cover in most of South Hornchurch.

Before the sewers were laid down, cesspools were used; in fact, cesspools were still being used by some homes in the 1930s. They were emptied by means of a horse and cart. It took a number of years to put in place a sewerage system throughout Hornchurch, but by the early part of the twentieth century most areas were covered.

Gas and Electricity

The Romford Gas and Coke Company was formed by deed of settlement to take over a small works at South Street, originally set up by Mr Bell in 1840. It became a limited company in 1874. It wasn't until about 1872 that the company extended its mains to Hornchurch. Many panicked about the 'new-fangled technology' in the early days, as explosions were alarmingly common, along with the risk of carbon monoxide poisoning. Street lighting took some time to be established. By January 1886 it was decided that the village and lane leading to the station should have twenty-five lamps, the cost to be met by a voluntary rate.

Residents of Emerson Park and Wingletye Lane were not part of the Hornchurch lighting area; they had a long wait before the Lighting and Watching Act of 1833 was accepted in their ward. The parish council had debated the situation for years. A meeting initially took place in 1901 to consider the question of street lighting for the Emerson Park estate – they were still debating it in 1912. At a parish meeting in May that year, Mr Townsend, a resident, objected to the proposal, saying he was one who lived in a little house and paid rent. He did not want to pay anything to help property owners to sell their houses. He said: 'Public lighting was not needed, because the incandescent lights in the

Hay Green, Nr Lilliputs, Wingletye Lane, *c.* 1950. (Upminster Tithe Barn)

houses illuminated the roads splendidly.' A vote resulted in twenty-nine for the proposal and thirty-two against. Some new houses were still being fitted with gas lighting in the early 1920s.

In 1913, the County of London Electric Supply Company was given statutory powers to supply much of south Essex, including Hornchurch. The First World War caused a major delay and Hornchurch did not receive electricity until shortly after Barking power station was opened in May 1925. By 1936 there were thirty-four sub-stations in the Hornchurch district and five others under construction. After years of using gas to light homes and the streets, electricity was seen as a boon.

Library Service

A main library for Hornchurch had been under discussion by the Hornchurch Urban District Council since the early 1930s. It petitioned Essex County Council, who provided library services in the county, and at a meeting on 15 October 1934, a recommendation was made to provide a service for Hornchurch. At its inaugural meeting at Langtons on 7 January 1935, the Hornchurch Branch Library Sub-Committee of the Essex County Council Education Committee, decided on a location – Harrow Lodge Farm. It wasn't ideal, as a more central position would have been better for residents, but it was the best they could find at the time. Space in Hornchurch Hall was also considered and rejected before the library opened in Harrow Lodge Farm on 12 October 1936, with a stock of 4,500 books.

Harrow Lodge, an eighteenth-century building that underwent various alterations.

Hornchurch Library, 2019.

Over the years, the location of the library was still debated, but it wasn't until 1953 that the main library moved to Fairkytes in Billet Lane. Harrow Lodge continued as a small branch library until 1965 when it was closed. Eventually, the decision was made to build a new library in North Street, and on 7 September 1967 the Mayor of Havering, William Sibley, officially opened the building – it opened to the public the following day. Thirty-nine years later, the library closed on 31 March 2006 so that it could be refurbished. It reopened in August 2007.

DID YOU KNOW?

Horses were prized possessions in the eighteenth century. On 25 June 1788, William Stevenson, aged nineteen, was found guilty at the Old Bailey for stealing a mare worth three guineas from John Manders of Hornchurch. He was given the death penalty, but this was later commuted to transportation to New South Wales, Australia, for a period of twenty-one years.

Bibliography

Mannox, Barbara, *Hornchurch and the New Zealand Connection* (London Borough of
    Havering, 1993)
Mannox, Barbara, *The Making of Emerson Park* (London Borough of Havering 1991)
Perfect, Charles Thomas, *Ye Olde Village of Hornchurch* (Benham & Company, 1917.
    Reprinted by Ian Henry Publications, 2005)
Powell, W. R., Volume VII of the *Victoria History of the County of Essex* (London Borough
    of Havering Libraries & Cultural Activities Department, 1988)

Image Source
Map of Hornchurch 1805 – Copyright (c) 2004–2015 of the Great Britain Historical GIS
Project and the University of Portsmouth. This work is licensed under the Creative
Commons Attribution 4.0 International License.

Acknowledgements

My thanks go to Simon Donoghue, local history librarian from Central Library, Romford, whose help has been invaluable. I would also like to thank the following people and organisations for their help in supplying information and images: Essex Field Club; Queen's Theatre; Hornchurch Aerodrome Historical Society; Essex Records Office; Purfleet Heritage Centre; Yad Vashem; Havering Museum, Romford; Fire Museum, Grays; Upminster Tithe Barn; and Judith Brooks, St Andrew's Church.